FROM GRANTS TO CONTRACTS

by

Keith Hawley

Goldsmiths
UNIVERSITY
OF LONDON

Centre for Public and Voluntary Sector Development

A joint NCVO/Directory of Social Change
Contract Culture publication

FROM GRANTS TO CONTRACTS

By **Keith Hawley**

Cover design by Nicholas Karides

First published by the Directory of Social Change with the
National Council for Voluntary Organisations, with financial
assistance from the Baring Foundation

ISBN 0-907164 83 8

Typeset by Jane Wood

Printed in Britain by Biddles of Guildford

Directory of Social Change, Radius Works, Back Lane,
London NW3 1HL. Tel. 071-284 4364

National Council for Voluntary Organisations,
Address from 1st June 1992: Regents Wharf, 8 All Saints
Street, London N1 9RL. Tel. 071-713 6161

Contents

Acknowledgements

Many people have played a part in the events leading to this publication and I thank them all. Special appreciation is however due to Leah for word-processing the original draft and to Kathy for her support and forbearance.

Introduction

Legislative changes throughout the 1980's gave a consistent message that the role of the State as a direct producer of goods and services was to be reduced. The Government's privatisation programme, the introduction of compulsory competitive tendering for certain local authority services and changes to the way health, housing, education and social services were delivered have taken us further towards the concept that state bodies enable things to happen and then monitor the results. They no longer do everything themselves.

This has created what is called the Contract Culture since contracts are now part of the mechanisms which local authorities and other statutory bodies use to secure the delivery of services. These are commissioned primarily from external providers but in some cases, from in-house suppliers too. The change which this has implied for both statutory and voluntary organisations has been profound. Neither had too much experience of a 'commercial' approach. To some extent, fear of the unknown and of that which is not understood has produced an over reaction to the changes and human beings are not at their best when they are in a state of panic and confusion. This book therefore tries to demystify the contract culture and enable it to be seen for what it is, merely a change in direction. It is written from a local authority's perspective primarily for the benefit of the voluntary sector, but it should also be useful to colleagues in the Health Authorities and other statutory 'purchasing' bodies.

The Contract Culture is about being specific about what needs to be done. About being clear about how what needs to be done, is to be done and about mechanisms for checking on the results.

Whilst it is important not to be over simplistic, if it fills its purpose, this will be a relatively simple book to read and use. It is also intended to give reassurance that contracting does not in fact imply contracting out of all statutory services and that in responding to the Contract Culture, local authorities do not need to abandon their traditional value base. They have a long tradition of public service and this is needed now as much as ever.

Local authorities are being asked by new legislation to become enablers. This means that they are being asked to help make things happen. Communities desperately need leadership and help to make things happen and voluntary organisations are important elements in communities. What is needed therefore, is a positive approach to contracting – to making things happen – and one which gives the voluntary sector both as providers of services and advocates for users a strong role in determining the outcomes.

Chapter One

This chapter looks at the rise and fall of the lamented 'Local Authority grants' culture. It implies that this was in fact a brief period in the evolution of voluntary activity and that to some extent, the increase in grant aid seen in the early 1980's was part of a process of change to which the Contract Culture was an inevitable conclusion.

Chapter Two

This chapter suggests that although a scene has been set by Government legislation and tone, the Contract Culture is in fact developing at a faster pace than legislation on its own demands.

It looks at the change agents operating in local authorities, and indicates that the springboard for change in a particular local authority can have a significant impact on how the contracting process develops.

Chapter Three

This chapter explains that once the statutory body has decided to conduct its relationships with voluntary bodies on a contractual basis, voluntary groups need to consider the implications for themselves. Statutory bodies too should be aware of these concerns. Both sectors should address the issues of the skill and expertise which is needed in the voluntary sector if voluntary organisations are to be enabled to enter into contracting confidently.

Chapter Four

This chapter identifies current patterns of relationships between voluntary organisations and local authorities and considers the kinds of changes within local authorities which will take place as a result of the development of contractual relationships. It looks at the differing arrangements that might be used and investigates the problems for managers with little previous experience of dealing with voluntary organisations or managing contracts. It calls attention to problems of relationship within local authorities, for example, with legal departments, treasurers departments and committee members and asks whether the experiences of compulsory competitive tendering with commercial suppliers will help or hinder an understanding of the local authority's requirements in developing sound arrangements with voluntary groups.

Chapter Five

This chapter looks in some detail at how specifications can

be developed. It is argued that these are the most important components of any contract and it is necessary for a full understanding to be developed of how they can be drawn up and what should be included.

Chapter Six
This chapter looks at the requirements on a voluntary organisation as a contractor. It suggests that local authorities will want reassurances that voluntary organisations are competent to manage and discusses areas in which their competencies may be put to the test.

Chapter Seven
This chapter suggests that local authorities commitments to the voluntary sector as contractors extend beyond the transfer of money. It suggests that local authorities should be enablers in the full sense of the word, recognising that voluntary organisations need access to a range of advice and support on financial, insurance, equal opportunities and personnel issues and looks at ways in which this can be provided.

Chapter Eight
This chapter looks at the monitoring processes which may be developed for reviewing the progress of contracts. It suggests that ongoing contract management is crucial and that the annual review should be more of a stock take producing few real surprises. It considers fair but firm mechanisms for evaluation and looks at self evaluation, quality assurance and the development of performance indicators.

Chapter Nine
This chapter summarises some of the essential messages of the book and reviews the processes which need to be developed for successful contracting with voluntary

organisations. It refers to a number of tools which have been used in Oxfordshire and which may be developed elsewhere and suggests further reading.

Chapter 1
The Rise and Fall of the Grants Culture

In the beginning

The expectation that voluntary organisations should be funded by grants from Central and Local Government is quite recent in evolutionary terms. Historically, charities and other voluntary organisations identified need, often in conjunction with the Church, and raised money from private benefactors to address it. Thousands of (parochial) parish charities still exist today and many of them will have started with a gift from an individual or a family. Typically this was to provide fuel or bread for the poor or shelter in the form of alms houses. Whilst many of these parish charities are now insignificant, where the original gift took the form of land they may be extremely wealthy. Similarly, many national voluntary organisations now seen as major service providers started because someone became concerned about a matter of social or educational deprivation or injustice and associated with others to address it. The Children's Society, formerly known as the Waifs and Strays, and the Royal National Institute for the Blind are organisations with such origins. The activities of these pioneers often included an element of campaigning for legislative reform and direct Government intervention. Many of the developments in public welfare policy over the past 100 years have been influenced by national voluntary organisations.

A Brief Age of Enlightenment?

The history of the UK is a history of a vibrant voluntary sector with visions of Utopia. It appeared for a time in the 1950's, however, that the need for the voluntary sector to render alms and provide direct care was perhaps a feature of the past.

The present and the future was to be about a Welfare State taking care of people's health, social and educational needs from the cradle to the grave. Comprehensive universal arrangements would be made by Central and Local Government to provide a guaranteed minimum level of financial support. Everyone would be entitled to free health care for each and any ailment. Education would be offered commensurate with an individual's ability to profit from it and would address both their personal and vocational needs. No one would be short of adequate housing.

This vision left little need for voluntary action which, of its essence, is patchy and incomplete. Voluntary organisations would continue to function, but their roles would be to identify areas of unmet need and pursue new ways of meeting them, in preparation for the state taking them into their own new welfare organisations. Voluntary organisations might also act as pressure groups or provide volunteers for the state; a few were actually given key tasks in the light of their specialist expertise. The National Society for the Prevention of Cruelty to Children had a continued remit to seek out cases of abuse of children and bring prosecutions. At the local level, church societies caring for blind and partially sighted people and those with hearing disabilities often continued to run their services as agents of the Local Authority.

The overall picture and expectation however was that in future the state would provide the services. These would be available as a civil right and they would be paid for out of rates and taxes.

Reality and Revision

This vision of Utopia unfortunately foundered on the rocks of a disparity, the disparity between the expectations which had been generated for a healthy life in full employment and with easy access to education and social services, and the reality of unemployment, long waiting lists for medical attention, poor educational standards and non existent community services for people who were homeless, elderly, physically or mentally disabled or mentally ill. The people blamed the government. The government blamed the culture of dependency which the Welfare State had generated. Both turned to the voluntary sector.

The people turned to the voluntary sector as they had in the past to meet needs which the state was not meeting. They turned to the voluntary sector to articulate to the state the claims for the welfare rights to which they now felt entitled. The state turned to the voluntary sector for solutions to a wide range of its problems, but most particularly to the problems of unemployment and housing.

In the early 1980's, rising unemployment was again a major challenge. This was seen by the Government to be a necessary and inevitable consequence of the major structural change in the economy which had to be achieved but they were anxious to seek short term solutions to keep people off the dole, reduce the level of unemployment and to enable people to continue to make a useful contribution to society. One such solution which was relatively cheap to implement was that of giving money to voluntary organisations to organise unemployed people into doing work of benefit to the community.

There were various ways of doing this including a community programme organised by the Manpower Services Commission and the Opportunities for Volunteering Fund organised through the National Council for Voluntary Organisations. The MSC Programme paid the wages of people engaged on community work whilst the Opportunities for Volunteering Fund supported the cost of selected voluntary organisations who were able to organise unemployed people into doing voluntary work. Whilst the money available was relatively small from the Government's point of view, it was in quite significant sums from the voluntary organisations perspective. Whilst many had misgivings that taking the money could distort their prime purposes and others feared that they might be compromising their ability to carry out campaigning roles, for many organisations the money was too tempting. They seized it partly because it was a way of fostering their own growth, but also because they felt unable to sit by whilst opportunities existed for providing useful occupations for people who were otherwise unemployed, occupations which would, at the same time, be providing services for people in need.

For some of those voluntary organisations which took part, and they included the great national organisations as well as many local groups, Community Programme money provided the first opportunity to become real service providers. As a result, a mini renaissance of voluntary organisations as providers of services gained momentum. Voluntary organisations came to be seen as an important vehicle for getting things done, a vehicle which seemed to have a number of advantages. Firstly, they were not the state, secondly they could act quickly, thirdly they could add value through the involvement of voluntary workers.

Voluntary Organisations : Providers Reinstated

Partly as a result of these Government Programmes therefore, the early 1980's saw considerable growth in the importance of voluntary organisations as managers of services and this suited the Governments policy objectives quite well since Mrs Thatcher's administrations sought to withdraw the state from industries and services which could be managed independently. Thus the growth of the voluntary sectors role in the management of provision was seen as extending the philosophy of creating more opportunities for exercising choice amongst users and competitiveness amongst suppliers. Some Local Authorities looked on in bemusement as Government subsidies were pumped into the local voluntary sectors and argued that they could have used the money better themselves. In some cases they undoubtedly could have but nevertheless they were swept along and to a large extent, embroiled. They were embroiled because they were often called upon to find the work for the community service employees to carry out. Of its nature, the tasks had to be simple and labour intensive. Environmental and social welfare projects were therefore high on every local MSC organisers agenda as the rush to fix jobs grew in volume. Local Authorities were also embroiled because they could be called upon to verify the credentials and management plans of voluntary organisations applying for grant aid from the national funds or because they had to assist with premises, training or part funding. Given the amount of unmet need in most areas, it was not easy for Local Authorities to refuse to cooperate with schemes which were popular and seen to be the only way of providing services regarded as essential. Once caught up in this, sometimes uneasy partnership with voluntary organisations however, Local Authorities found difficulty in disentangling themselves. In some cases they had given a commitment to continue funding when Government grants ran out.

In other situations the services provided through the voluntary organisation had become well established and Local Authorities were willing to recognise that the service being provided was worth maintaining. In other areas, negative factors prevailed; it would have just been too unpopular for Local Authorities not to continue to support organisations which had developed political influence and attachment. The corollary however was that many voluntary organisations had grown rapidly and had become well and truly dependent upon the grant aid which they were receiving from Central and Local Government. They had often built up substantial work forces of paid staff and had gone way beyond the point where charitable giving or fund raising could make more than a marginal contribution to what they needed in order to sustain themselves.

Grants and Rights

For a brief, perhaps all too brief period, it may have seemed to some voluntary organisations that the public purse was there for the taking. There was money from the Manpower Services Commission, money from the Opportunities for Volunteering Fund, Section 11 grants for work with ethnic minorities, grants from the Home Office, Urban Aid, grants from Joint Finance, grants from Local Authorities, for organisations in London grants from the GLC and for Housing Associations through the Housing Corporation.

Some of the examples to illustrate this trend are quite dramatic. Housing Associations became more significant providers of public housing than Local Authorities. National voluntary organisations developed job creation schemes which had a bigger turnover than the parent organisation itself.

New voluntary organisations were created over night as a vehicle for a job creation scheme. For example, in Banbury, Oxfordshire one small self-help organisation for the parents of children with special needs became an employer of a dozen staff who then did the helping.

The arrangements for awarding this money were often quite unsophisticated; success depending more on an ability to get a proposal ready quickly to meet short deadlines or effective lobbying, than on well considered, well costed and carefully argued proposals. Monitoring arrangements were poorly developed, concentrating more on ensuring that money was not embezzled than that it was effectively used. Voluntary organisations for their part began to take state aid for granted, led by a conviction of the validity and soundness of their mission and encouraged by easily won support, often sustained by vacuous and indiscriminate praise for their efforts by figures in public life. Some voluntary organisations came to see themselves as having a priority call on public money and grant aid as a natural right. They were ripe for disappointment.

The National Agenda

Whilst voluntary organisations clearly had a part set out for them in the dominant political ideology of the 1980's, it was in fact a small part when set against the whole. Government policy in the 1980's was firmly directed at restructuring the public sector. Ideas reminiscent of nineteenth century *laissez-faire* Liberalism were on the loose and conviction abounded that the state had grown too dominant and overbearing and that its power and influence over economic and social life should be curbed.

Reports from various think-tanks and the voice of the Audit Commission supported these convictions and indicated how the process of developing a more pluralistic consumer orientated society should be pursued.

Local Government

One main target was Local Government, which was seen as being weakly and ineffectively managed, and where in some places elected councillors were believed to be pursuing ideology at the expense of the ratepayers interests. The public was seen as having lost confidence in the standard of services and answers were seen in terms of creating greater accountability of Local Authorities to their electors. The Poll

Tax was part of the mechanism for this. Another part was to lie in exposing Local Authority services to more competition.

Measures for achieving this through loosening a local authority's grip on direct service provision included:

* The 1988 Local Government Act which introduced Compulsory Competitive Tendering for a range of services such as refuse collection, grounds maintenance and cleaning.

* Restriction of Local Authorities ability to build new homes

* Incentives to encourage tenants to buy the homes they lived in

* Legislation to allow independent organisations such as housing associations to buy whole housing estates for improvement

* Schools to be allowed to control their own budget and to opt out of the control of Local Authorities altogether if they wish to do so

* Sports and leisure facilities later added to the list of activities to be compulsory tendered for with consideration being given to the addition of legal and accountancy services.

Community Care

Perhaps the most significant change in Local Government affecting relationships with the voluntary sector however are the changes to the way in which care for elderly, mentally ill, physically handicapped people, and people with learning difficulties will be provided. The changes were announced in response to the Griffith Report of 1988. This report had pointed to a need for change for a number of reasons including:

* A huge increase in Social Security payments to people in private and voluntary homes from approximately £20

million in 1979/80 to nearly £1 billion in 1988/89.

* At the same time, Local Authority expenditure on Social Services grew by only 30%, creating a gross imbalance. There was far more money for institutional care than Community Care.

* The need for a planned approach to welfare provision in the light of the increased numbers of elderly people in the population and increasing numbers of people with disabilities who were demanding a right to lead more normal lives.

* The need for greater consistency in planning and organising services between various Local Authority services and those of Health Authorities, Housing Associations and voluntary organisations.

* The need to simplify systems and ensure that users had more rights to be heard and to make choices about the services to be provided for them.

Governments Proposals

The Governments response was the White Paper - Caring for People and the subsequent NHS and Community Care Act which included provision to:-

* Develop community services which would enable people to live in their own homes wherever feasible and sensible.

* Ensure that those caring as family members, friends or neighbours should have their needs taken into account in meeting the needs of users

* Ensure that needs should be properly assessed and provision designed in line with the needs and preferences of the user.

* Ensure that Local Authorities should enable a strong independent sector to emerge in order to increase the range of options available for users who wish to exercise

consumer choice.

* Be clear about the responsibilities of various agencies so that they could be held more accountable for their performance.

Strong themes to emerge therefore were that the new arrangements for Community Care must depend upon consultation with users and their carers, the development of a mixed economy of providers and the need for strong structures to make providers accountable for the quality and effectiveness of the services which they provide.

Target – National Health Service

Another target has been the National Health Service where the reforms have also led to the service being split into 'purchasers' and 'providers' with a view to developing a market economy in health care.

Hospitals have been given opportunities to adopt self managing Trust status which means that they bid with each other for contracts from the Health Authorities. GP's were put on contracts which included performance related pay, and many given the opportunity to manage their own budgets. The intention being that market forces would bring down costs and improve quality.

Need for a New Vocabulary

The changes we have been describing are dramatic in the extreme. The 1980's saw a fundamental challenge to assumptions which had not been questioned since the Second World War. They were that health, education, housing and social welfare provision was a responsibility of the state and that services should be provided universally to all according to their need. Coupled with this had been a belief that these services could best be administered by professionals under political control who subscribed to a public service ethic and could usually therefore be relied upon to deliver effective services free from corruption.

Against these assumptions was a new ideology. An ideology which NCVO has described as the ideology of the Contract Culture. Its tenets are:

1. That public service provision has been found wanting.

2. That service provision should be consumer led rather than producer led.

3. That competition in a market economy provides a more effective mechanism for reducing costs and improving quality.

4. That funding relationships based on contracts are better than more informal partnerships.

5. That a more diverse and pluralistic pattern of service provision provides the consumer with a greater choice than monopolistic provision through local authorities or the state.

6. That the private and the voluntary sector are likely to provide better provision.

This is the ideology which now dominates decisions about Local Government, though it is not uncontested. Those who work in Local Government and those voluntary organisations who seek a relationship with it therefore need to learn its vocabulary.

* Purchaser/Commissioner
The purchaser has the money and the spending power. The purchaser buys or commissions services. In this scenario the purchaser may also be known as the client or the client-side.

* Provider/Contractor
The provider actually manages the service which the purchaser may buy or commission. Since the service is usually provided through a contract, the provider may also be known as the contractor.

* Service Specification
A Service Specification details what the service is about. It indicates what is to be provided, to what standard and quantity, to whom it must be provided for, when it will be provided and how what is provided will be monitored. The specification is drawn up by the purchaser who in the best of circumstances will do so in consultation with users and prospective contractors.

* The Contract
The contract is the document which records the agreement between the purchaser and provider about the specification for the service to be delivered and the arrangements for delivering it and paying for it. The contract also details the arrangements for monitoring the contract and for terminating it. It may be called a Service Agreement, a Grant Agreement, a Partnership Agreement or indeed something else again. It might even be called a Contract! A contract should always be regarded as legally binding although interestingly enough, there are one or two authorities and voluntary organisations who have written into their agreements that they are not to be regarded as legally binding!

* Tendering
Often when a purchaser wishes to enter into a contract to get a service delivered, the purchaser will draw up a specification and invite potential contractors to tender for it. This means the contractors are asked to indicate that they wish to provide the service and to say what the price would be. This process is called tendering.

* Competitive Tendering
When two or more contractors are invited to tender for the same contract, then they are in competition with each other usually on the basis of price and the process may be called competitive tendering.

* Compulsory Competitive Tendering
Compulsory Competitive Tendering must be distinguished

from competitive tendering since it only arises if the Government determines that a particular activity *must* be offered for tender on a competitive basis.

In this case, the process must be carried out in accordance with statutory regulations as indeed must all public tendering activity.

* Contract Monitoring
This is a process carried out by the purchaser to verify that a service is being provided by the contractor according to the contract specification.

A New Culture

This then is some of the vocabulary of contracting; the vocabulary of the contract culture. Clearly if the state is to retain responsibility for ensuring that certain levels of provision of health, education and social services are to be available but intend that this should not be provided directly by Government or Local Government organisations then some other system of management and control is necessary.

What we are discussing therefore is the mechanism by which this management and control of the providing of services takes place. It implies a very different system of state organisation to that which existed in the decades following the Second World War. The Welfare State as generally perceived assumed that government would make all the arrangements. Large organisations developed to administer and develop the system and although they were seen to suffer from the inherent problems of large bureaucracies, on the whole they were accepted as doing their best within the resources made available to them.

Essentially, the ideology of the Contract Culture provides that a culture of administration and service delivery in public affairs should give way to a culture of management and that what essentially needs to be managed is the process by which the use of Government money is prioritised and then spent in purchasing services which the consumer wants and which are produced effectively and economically. Who produces the service is not so important provided that the development of a monopoly position is not encouraged since that would lead to a new complacency with a likely commensurate drift in quality and price.

Contracts play a significant part in this thinking since they focus the minds of those involved either as purchasers or providers on a sharp analysis of what is involved or entailed in a process of producing a service. It is important to research what needs to be provided. It is important to analyse how it will be provided and how much it will cost. It is important to check that what is being produced is being produced efficiently and without waste and it is important to know that this has happened.

Is Contracting Out Inevitable?

Because of the strong lead given to the Contract Culture by the 1988 Act and Compulsory Competitive Tendering, it is often implied that the Contract Culture implies that all goods and services which the state needs to secure should, of necessity, be provided by an external contractor, that is contracted out. This need not be so. The contracting process can be seen as follows:

* Identify need, involving users if possible.
* Draw up specification based on those needs, involving contractor if one has been identified.
* Negotiate a contract.
* Contract Management, monitoring and review.

The primary benefits of the process are that it forces a clear identification of the need for which this service is to be designed and ensures that care is taken over the service design itself. That economy becomes a criteria for ordering the service and that the contractor of the service is carefully monitored to ensure that the service contracted is being delivered in accordance with the specification. This process can be applied equally well to a service provider within a local authority as one which is external to it and if there is a possibility that a contract for providing the service may be offered externally, then this, of itself, creates tension for the in-house provider which will make this provider act very similarly to the external provider. In other words, the very possibility that a service can be carefully designed and costed against a price offered externally will lead the in-house provider to ensure that their own costs and effectiveness are competitive.

Insofar as local and national government is becoming aware of what it costs to provide goods and services, this must be beneficial to those, who as tax and Council tax payers, pay for such services and for those who rely on them as users. If the contract culture, therefore, does not imply a culture where public services must always be contracted out it does imply a culture where costs and quality are known and where there must be a fairly determined and continual effort to improve effectiveness.

It may seem ironic to voluntary organisations that the changing climate which, in the early 1980's, initially made them the willing recipients of a cash bonanza offered without too much structure eventually evolved into one where the mechanisms for transferring cash to the voluntary sector became very structured indeed. This in turn has provided voluntary organisations who wish to become, or remain, part of the system of state-funded service provision with a major challenge. It is that of demonstrating that their own systems can be competitive and that whilst retaining the values and commitment which distinguishes them from the statutory and private sectors they can be businesslike and effective in managing themselves and their services.

Chapter 2
How Local Authorities decide to Contract

Although the political climate and legislative pressures may be pushing in the direction of contracting, the pace at which it is being introduced varies considerably from place to place. Some authorities want to be seen as contracting authorities; others seem to hope that it will all go away; most are somewhere in between, changing gradually at a rate which reflects the push of legislation and the ability of the authority's structure to take the strain. There will however be no change without someone or some force initiating it. Such agents for change have included the 1988 Local Government Act, management reviews, political conviction and finally departmental restructuring to meet the requirements of the Community Care Act.

The 1988 Act and Compulsory Competitive Tendering

The 1988 Local Government Act provided the Government with the power to introduce compulsory competitive tendering, CCT, for defined Local Authority activities. The Act specified some initial activities which were to be included. They were the collection of refuse, cleaning, catering, ground maintenance and the repair and maintenance of vehicles. Since the initial list sports and leisure facilities have been added and it is possible that professional services such as legal advice, architectural services and financial management may also be included.

Restructuring for C.C.T.

If an activity has been designated for CCT and the Local Authority wishes to continue to provide the service directly itself, they have to put the service out to competitive tender and the Council's own operation and workforce must bid against private or voluntary sector bidders who want to take the work over. The effect of this has been that Local Authorities had to restructure the activity so that it could operate independently from the rest of the Council. This process imparted two disciplines, one a purchaser discipline and the other a provider discipline.

The Purchasers

On the purchasing or client side, a Council had to decide who was to be responsible for drawing up a precise specification for the service which the Council needed to buy. They also had to develop the skills and expertise to do it. For example, the specification for a cleaning contract could involve measuring all areas to be cleaned and determining to what standard they had to be cleaned, how often, with what materials and within what constraints. Schools clearly can not be cleaned during the school day. This was a new exercise for most councils and entailed a considerable amount of detailed and painstaking work. They had problems in deciding which members of staff that had previously been involved in providing the service was in future to be involved in commissioning or purchasing it. This was not an easy task since there may have been very few people actually involved in managing the service at the top level and whilst preparations were being made for the purchaser/provider future, the ongoing work of running the activity was still necessary.

The Providers

The provider discipline was equally rigorous. The Local Authority had to assign people to plan a shadow organisation which was to bid for the future contract. This meant learning new skills and taking a new approach to costings. The work force which hoped to successfully bid for the contract had to re-think its working practices, terms and conditions of service and form different assumptions about the future. A job in the Local Authority had previously been seen as a job for life, these workers faced the reality that if they did not win their contract, they would be redundant unless a successful bidder decided to take them on. The work force thus had to learn about the competitive process and in formulating their own bid price, take account of likely bids from competitors.

Compulsory Competitive Tendering – An Agent for Change

Compulsory Competitive Tendering had an immediate and profound effect on the Authorities affected by it. They had to learn a new approach to their activities very quickly. Everything had to be costed and subjected to market forces. In most local authorities the true costs of an operation were not really known because they were spread throughout the Authority. Legal departments, treasurers departments, personnel departments, public relations departments etc., usually served all sections and the time and other costs associated with these activities were not easily divided amongst the Councils specific service operations. Similarly many local authorities did not know the cost of the space which they occupied. Competitive Tendering for contracts was therefore sometimes perceived as a discipline which had a value all of its own and which could usefully be introduced into other areas of service provision even though there was no immediate compulsion to do so.

Management Reviews

The 1980's, particularly the second part of the decade, saw a new breed of manager moving into key positions in Local Government management. Although many of them had a background in Local Government, they had had a different kind of training, often in business school, and they brought a different kind of approach. They were enthusiastic about the change of political ideology and committed to managing rather than administering. They wanted proaction rather than reaction. They were prepared to challenge traditional ways of doing things. They were not afraid of the media and wished to encourage a closer relationship with consumers of Local Government services. Whilst mindful of the political constraints under which they operated, they believed that by developing a dialogue with their public, by gaining public support for the services which they offered, they would create an environment where it was easier for the politicians to give them the resources which they needed to develop better services.

This breed of manager was versed in the need for setting clear objectives, specifying requirements and standards and developing processes for monitoring how effectively the organisation was being managed. Not surprisingly, one of the first measures which such managers adopted was to review the way their departments were operating. What they often found was confusion, fog and great difficulty in determining who was doing what, for what purpose and at what cost. A relatively easy target initially was to look at grant aid to the voluntary sector. In some Authorities substantial sums of money were spent on grants with very little control or monitoring of the process. The new managers wanted to know precisely what this money was being used for and more particularly wanted to know too if it could be redirected to other priorities.

A Typical Grants Process

When these new managers looked, what they often found was a process where voluntary organisations would make an annual application for grant aid. They would do this on a form provided by the Authority and it would then be processed by an administrator who would probably ask for accounts and a copy of an annual report. All these facts would then be compiled into a report and put before a Committee of Members. Members would often make their decision on the basis of personal knowledge of the organisation, as a result of lobbying, from brief reports from Officers often produced on the basis of the grant application itself, or because it sounded a noble cause and to oppose it would appear churlish and lacking in community spirit. A significant factor in receiving grant aid was often that an organisation had received it before, but what it may have done with a previous grant was seldom examined in any great detail and few Authorities had either the will or the resources to introduce effective monitoring processes.

In these circumstances the review of grant aid often led to decisions that in the future grant aid would be more carefully targeted and that it would be more carefully controlled. One quite effective way of controlling it was by introducing Contracts or Service Agreements. These meant that the voluntary organisation and the local authority had to agree a specification for the service to be provided by the voluntary organisation in return for commitments about financial and other support from the local authority. In fact, most of the Contracts which currently exist with voluntary organisations have been introduced as a direct alternative to a grant which the organisation was previously receiving.

Political Pressure

In a democracy the role of elected members is of primary importance in determining how Local Authorities will behave. Issues around contracting have been quite emotive because of the association of contracting with Compulsory Competitive Tendering. Not only has CCT been seen as interference with the right of Local Authorities to determine their own affairs, but also as a mechanism for promoting privatisation of Local Authority services and thus the demise of the role of a Local Authority as a direct provider of services.

In some Authorities therefore, such as Bromley, where there is a strong political commitment towards privatisation or contracting out, there has been an impetus to go beyond the specified services for CCT and look at other options for subjecting services to market forces and to seek to make arrangements to contract others out if possible. In other Authorities, there has been total resistance to privatisation and little beyond the absolute minimum prescribed by law has been undertaken. It seems likely that where contracting is closely associated in members minds with contracting out, opportunities to evaluate the benefits of contracting as a process have not been pursued.

Is Contracting a Political Issue?

The use of contracts to regulate the partnership between Local Authorities and voluntary organisations was in fact commended in 1981 by a Working Party convened by the Association of Metropolitan Authorities, the National Council for Voluntary Organisations and the Association of County Councils.

Their report, 'Working Together, partnerships in local Social Services' stated:

1. "One valuable approach to grant aid is the establishment

of formal agreements which may or may not take the form of contracts.

2. Contracts can overcome some of the problems arising from short term funding arrangements.

3. A Contract will contain the elements of the relationships between the two approaches.

4. Some voluntary organisations may see a Contract as a restriction of their freedom to engage in activities not covered by the Contract. We do not share these fears.

5. Contracts do not create mutual trust, rather they are the product of such trust".

It is arguable that if attempts to change grant aid to voluntary organisations into contractual arrangements had been introduced as a response to the Working Party's report, rather than introduced in the context of a climate created by Competitive Tendering, it would not have become the emotive issue that it is at the present time.

There would of course still have been a need to ensure that contracting did not work to the disadvantage of small, less structured groups or those without ready access to professional expertise.

Departmental Restructuring

In the fast moving world of the 1980's and 1990's, any organisation needs to be flexible and able to change to deal with new realities. In Local Government, the realities have been the need to cope with increasing statutory responsibilities in the face of shrinking real resources and increasing Central Government control.

Local Authorities therefore have needed to become much sharper at identifying costs and re-ordering priorities, they have had to learn to manage as well as to administer and in turn, they have been exhorted to be responsive to the customer. The introduction of the poll tax was specifically aimed at increasing awareness in the minds of the charge payer of the cost of Local Government with a view to forcing local authorities to be more accountable to those who paid them for their services. Thus, restructuring has been inevitable as Authorities have struggled to streamline management and develop a more individual sense of responsibility in their staffs in order to speed up responsiveness.

As an example of this, Oxfordshire County Council launched its Quest Programme. Quest stands for Quality Effectiveness and Service to All. The programme was intended to make all departments re-examine the standards which they set for their services, to look at the effectiveness with which they delivered them and to ensure that the services were at all times customer orientated.

Double Guessing the Future

Restructuring in many Authorities has anticipated the future. Some County, District, or Borough Councils have assumed that exhortations to move towards becoming enabling Authorities may become more directive. In some cases therefore, authorities have tried to order themselves in such a way that if freedom to provide services directly is eroded and if through the extension of Compulsory Competitive Tendering or other mechanisms, they are forced to commission services from the voluntary and private sectors, they will have a structure which will be conducive to them doing this efficiently and effectively.

Such Authorities have therefore identified which parts of their organisation structure would act as the purchaser and which parts would continue to carry out provider roles. Clearly where these distinctions have been made, an impetus has been created internally for the providers to see themselves as at arms length from the rest of the organisation and for the purchasing sides to develop fairly vigorous approaches to specification, monitoring, inspection and cost effectiveness. This has been done in various ways, Berkshire appears to have divided itself clearly down the middle, other authorities have been less radical establishing discrete services such as transport, residential homes or the home care service as identifiable businesses. A few authorities have not been radical at all and purchaser and provider roles have been carried simultaneously by managers at varying levels.

Where such an impetus exists, it is easy to see how an enthusiasm for being effective in the purchasing role can overcome any corporate sense of commitment to being a direct provider of the service. Competition and assertiveness are likely to become driving forces irrespective of whether the potential provider is an in-house contractor or one from outside. Old allegiances die quickly as the new culture captures and excites the imagination.

NHS and Community Care Acts 1990

Local Authorities with a responsibility for Social Services are given a strong impetus to become fully paid up members of the Contract Culture through this legislation.

It gives wide-ranging responsibilities for organising the future care arrangements for elderly people, those who are physically or mentally disabled people, and those with problems with drugs or alcohol. Whilst transferring to the local authorities monies which have previously been expended by the Department of Social Security on supporting people in residential establishments, it also gives strong direction to how this money should be used. The guidance is insistent that it should be used to develop a mixed economy of care and that it would be unacceptable for local authorities to spend the extra cash on simply developing its own direct provider operations.

Community Care Plans

Local authorities must, in consultation with users, carers and the voluntary organisations which represent and support them, produce their care plans. These will be produced annually and will detail levels of need with indications of how it will be met. These plans must specifically indicate how services will be managed and what steps local authorities intend to take to widen choice for users.

Care Management and Assessment

The corner stone for the future is that local authorities should develop systems for assessing the needs of those who rely upon the local authority for support and then appoint a Care Manager who, in consultation with the users and his/her carers, will design a package of measures to meet the needs revealed by the assessment. Assessment and care management can be seen as the primary purchasing function but what has yet to be determined are the vital mechanisms by which local authorities determine how much is available for the care managers to spend, both in total and for a particular client.

Most local authorities have yet to determine whether the care managers will actually have a sum of money to use at their own discretion or whether they will only have a claim against services provided by other local authority staff or purchased in bulk from operators in the voluntary or the private sector.

Commissioning and Purchasing

Many local authorities have yet to develop their approach to commissioning and purchasing and although they may have been consulted about the options, it is about the outcomes that the voluntary sector waits expectantly to hear. There is no predetermined mix of services as yet, but it is clear that unless local authorities do of their own volition choose to buy in the market place, further Government action may force them to do so.

In developing their commissioning and purchasing strategies, local authorities have many difficult decisions to make. They have to decide which suppliers in the independent sector they want to deal with and the criteria for selecting them out. They have to decide what forms of contracts they should use, whether they should be formal and rather aloof or whether more partnership based. They have to decide whether to go for block or bulk contracts and if so what arrangements to make to call off them or whether to go more for 'spot' buying for one person's needs at a time. If they buy in block or bulk, then stability will be provided for at least part of the independent market place but they tie themselves in for long periods to those organisations which they have block contracts with. If they go 'spot' then the market place is kept extremely volatile with less security on both sides.

Independent Inspection

The Community Care Act also requires local authorities to establish independent inspection units which must be responsible for the standards of care provided not only in the independent sector but also by the in-house providers. These inspection units must act independently of the department itself and it seems likely that their scope and powers will grow. They will become part of the mechanism for ensuring that all providers, whether local authority, private or voluntary, operate services to acceptable quality standards.

Complaints Procedures

The Act also requires Social Services departments to appoint Complaints Officers and to develop complaints procedures to enable users to understand their rights and to know how to complain and seek redress if they do not believe that they are receiving an adequate service.

Summary

In short, the processes of assessment, care management and the development of commissioning and purchasing process means that local authorities will have to separate the processes for running services from those of determining who should use them. The Community Care Plan makes it visible how this is done and will provide a mechanism for independent sector providers to ascertain whether they are being given a fair opportunity to share in the market for care. The inspection units will be there to ensure that standards of quality are being universally applied throughout the sector and by giving a higher profile to complaints procedures will be part of the process of engaging users in passing critical judgement on how effective the service to them is becoming.

Coping with Change

The process of change within a Local Authority is likely to be quite traumatic, both for its own staff and for those outside agencies that it needs to relate to. These relationships of course include voluntary organisations. It is important therefore that the local authorities enter into a dialogue with those likely to be concerned. As with other changes, a change to contracting will entail encountering and resolving problems, the character of which can not necessarily be understood in advance. The development of a climate of trust is essential and so is the necessity of setting good ground rules because otherwise things could go seriously wrong. There are examples of doubtful and better practices already available.

Example One

Some Authorities have chosen to pilot contracting with one or two voluntary organisations to "get the feel" of it and see what is involved. The intentions may have been sound but the consequences have sometimes been bitter. Those organisations chosen have been unsure about why they have been chosen. There has been fear that they may have been selected for closer scrutiny and monitoring, perhaps because the Local Authority was seeking evidence for cutting off the money to them altogether. This has been the case in particular if the contracts offered have only been for one year in length thus producing no perceived financial advantage over grant aid. Yet those organisations who have not been chosen have worried that they may be the ones which are not regarded as important. They have been angered that perhaps decisions about future grant aid are being taken privately and that perhaps the Local Authority and some parts of the voluntary sector are in collusion.

The consequential division caused within the voluntary movement in a particular area where this has occurred means that it is likely to take an essentially negative attitude to Contracting in general and any benefits from the process therefore become more difficult to extract.

Example Two

Another difficulty has been where contracting has been initiated by Officers without Member involvement. It must be anticipated that voluntary groups will have reservations about contracting. This is in fact confirmed by the level of concern that has been expressed at local level across the country and nationally. Voluntary organisations are often fairly well connected with members and naturally enough, members will be amongst the first to hear of their concerns. If the first that members of a particular authority hear of contracts being offered or considered is when voluntary organisations complain to them, the members are likely to round on the officers who they feel should have consulted with them. Tension may therefore be created within the authority itself between officers and members. A trail of negative emotions can be generated which may in turn be displaced upon the contract process itself and by officers towards the voluntary sector which they may feel has misjudged their intentions.

Example Three

In authorities where the process has been open and where voluntary organisations have had the opportunity to influence it, a different ethos has been created.

By consulting widely with voluntary organisations about their intentions, local authorities have been able to let voluntary organisations use their own creative energy to shape the process and they have therefore identified with it and partnership has grown as a result.

The Contract Culture in Oxfordshire

In Oxfordshire the arrival of a new Director, anxious to review all aspects of the workings of the Social Services Department prompted the development of a move from a Grants to a Contracts Culture. This was carried out in a number of stages. The first stage was a discussion paper to the Social Services Committee explaining that changes were afoot and arguing that in the future the County Council would need to carefully identify which voluntary organisations it needed to work in partnership with. These organisations would need to be strengthened and secured.

It would be important to be clear about what they were doing for the money they were receiving so a specification would be drawn up against which future performance would be monitored.

The benefits to the Local Authority would be clarity about and security for the continuation of an important service. The benefits for a voluntary organisation would be clarity but also security of funding over a longer period than twelve months. The discussion paper concluded with the recommendation that more detailed proposals should be brought to a future meeting of the Committee for a decision in principle upon which Officers could consult with the voluntary sector. This was agreed but because the issues had been well publicised at this, the first stage, voluntary organisations knew what was afoot and where able to contribute towards the development of the officers thinking. The proposals which officers recommended to the Committee as a basis for consultation with the voluntary sector were therefore, in a sense, themselves the product of some consultation.

The proposals to the committee where that for the future support to the voluntary sector should take three forms.

Firstly, organisations that provided cost effective services which formed an alternative to direct Local Authority provision would be given Service Agreements which would provide for a clear specification, monitoring, review and a guarantee of funding over three years. Such payments would no longer be regarded as grants from the Social Services Grants Budget but would be seen as part and parcel of the basic budget for delivering services. Any reports would therefore go back direct to the Social Services Committee itself.

The second category was support to organisations in the voluntary sector which supported other voluntary organisations. Many of these groups also had staff and needed security of funding. Their role was crucial to the development of a contracting process because they were the organisations which offered support, advice and encouragement to the rest of the voluntary sector.

They were strategically important therefore, both in their support role and because of the help which they could give to other organisations in negotiating agreements with the Local Authority. These organisations would also be monitored against a specification and given three year Service Agreements. Their money would not be transferred from the grants budget however and the Grants Sub Committee would continue to receive reports about them and be responsible for their future welfare.

The third category recognised that there was a continuing need for grant aid to support smaller organisations to encourage new developments and to provide an avenue of assistance to organisations which were not directly service providers or local development agencies.

Consultation Process

The consultation process around these proposals was jointly planned with the Council for Voluntary Action and took a number of forms. First, there was a rather grand conference addressed by the Director of Social Services and attended by Senior Officers of the department and by Chief Officers of voluntary organisations. This conference gave a cautious approval to the proposals in principle but established Working Groups to look at the detail and to consider what service agreements should look like and how they should be negotiated and ultimately monitored and implemented.

The next level of consultation therefore was done through smaller conferences, workshops and working groups which tried to identify the issues to be addressed. The Council for Voluntary Action played an invaluable role in coordinating this activity.

At the same time, Officers of the department were talking to organisations who wanted the opportunity of a more confidential discussion of how the process was likely to affect them. It was important to engage in this dialogue because it enabled more parts of the voluntary sector to play a constructive role in the wider debate and therefore identify with the ultimate outcome. It also helped to clarify specific worries and doubts which organisations privately nursed. As a result of this consultative process over a twelve week period, the Director of Social Services was able to go back to his Committee in June 1989 and recommend that the switch to Contracting should begin from the following financial year and that the organisations to receive the early contracts should be identified forthwith.

Not surprisingly, most of the first group of contractors were organisations already in receipt of grant aid or in receipt of support known locally as Agency support. Agency Support was given to a number of organisations who, for one reason or another, had been allocated funding on an ongoing basis.

Payments to Organisations

The way was now clear for officers to talk to organisations about their individual agreements. It was made clear that if at the end of the day an organisation did not feel comfortable with the service agreement and did not want to sign one, that they would not rule themselves out for consideration of an annual grant as before. It seemed important that all organisations being offered service agreements should be offered an agreement which was consistent with the rest and to facilitate this, a checklist was drawn up again in consultation with the voluntary sector and used as the basis for agreements. This checklist was used flexibly and subsequently amended as experience developed.

Chapter 3

Implications for Voluntary Organisations

Voluntary organisations in the United Kingdom are not used to contracts. Many are used to providing services and to providing these in conjunction with statutory bodies but usually this has been done with grant aid. In this context, a grant should be seen as a gift and indeed recipients have usually seen their relationship with their local authority's supporters as one whereby they receive a gift to enable them to carry out their purpose. The voluntary organisations purpose is identified by the local authority as its own purpose and forms an essential bond of kinship.

Contracts are not quite the same. If voluntary organisations are to develop as state-funded service providers, the mechanism to administer this is likely to be contracts. Yet the local authorities themselves must take into account the realities of the voluntary sector. In the UK it is very diverse and its managerial capacity varies considerably. Many national and some local voluntary organisations are strong and well resourced, but if they are to maximise on the richness and variety of the voluntary sector local authorities will also have to find ways of dealing with organisations which are not so well structured or managed but where nevertheless the benefits of the voluntary sectors participation in service provision will be worthwhile. Many voluntary organisations may be less well structured on their management sides precisely because of an overriding concern about their value systems and the need for openness to influence from the community which they see as their constituency.

Local Authorities should therefore be aware of the constraints and the concerns within the voluntary sector about participating in the contracting process and consider how far they can go to help the voluntary sector deal with them. Many of these concerns have been well documented by the National Council for Voluntary Organisations and in this chapter we shall look at some of them.

Mission

A voluntary organisation's mission is its reason for existence. Its mission will indicate its value system and it is probably its mission which distinguishes it most clearly from organisations operating in the private sector where profit is the goal.

Voluntary organisations may be concerned that a contract will lure them away from their essential mission and this fear may be well founded in experiences in the early 1980's when the easy availability of Government funding for certain purposes, for example, the Community Programme, led organisations to bid for it because it was there. As a result, many organisations felt that they had been diverted into furthering statutory missions rather than their own. Local authorities should not ignore this dimension and should explore honestly with a voluntary organisation whether the tasks which the statutory body are seeking to have carried out do fit comfortably with the objectives which the voluntary organisation believes it is established to pursue. Failure to establish this degree of mutual respect at the beginning can lead to difficulties later.

A successful Council for Voluntary Service which had a good record for attracting and deploying volunteers co-ordinating voluntary organisations and fostering the development of new groupings was asked by its local authority to set up and manage a furniture project. The local authority was concerned at the number of people who did not have furniture and were prepared to provide money to the CV for them to organise the collection of surplus furniture from people who were prepared to give it away, store it and recycle it to people who needed it. This was an attractive proposition, one which the CV correctly thought would bring it into credit with the local authority and so they agreed to go ahead. The service was popular and grew in size.

Unfortunately, the effort of managing the project started to divert the Organising Secretary from his other tasks. Instead of co-ordinating voluntary groups and providing an information and advice service to affiliated organisations, he spent his time supporting the furniture store Project Manager who was over worked and could not cope with the multitude of tasks related to the furniture project. The local authority was unable to provide any further financial help. The Director tried to prioritise but then people who wanted to give furniture were disgusted that the Council could not arrange to take it away whilst people who wanted furniture queued up and even fought for what was available. Meanwhile the member organisations who used to telephone the office in vain, became concerned that they were not getting the help which they needed and that the effectiveness of the CUS was becoming less effective at speaking on behalf of the voluntary sector.

Independence

Voluntary organisations are concerned that a contract could threaten their independence. This is related to the issue about their mission but is distinct from it. It is particularly likely that if a voluntary organisation has previously been grant aided by the local authority, to pursue its general purposes, the voluntary organisation will feel under threat when the local authority seeks to be more specific about why the money is being given. The voluntary organisation may well feel that it is being taken over by the statutory body and simply being regarded as an agent.

This perceived threat to a voluntary organisation may be particularly acute where it acts both as a local development agency and as a service provider. Age Concern groups often fall into this category.

In a particular county, the countywide Age Concern Organisation provides support to a wide variety of local Age Concern groups, elderly people's clubs, pensioners associations, in fact several dozen organisations concerned with providing help to elderly people. It also fosters new initiatives such as groups organising gardening and decorating for elderly people, insulation of homes, community education classes and holiday fellowship groups. It has been very successful in its general role of developing and supporting this community effort, both involving and on behalf of elderly people. In addition, it runs three day centres and a granny and grandad respite sitting service. When the local authority gave grant aid, it did not ask how it was being used, it simply gave it to the support of Age Concern activities. When the authority switched to contracting however, it focused on the day centres and the respite care scheme and was concerned to develop a specification which would have cost more to implement than Age Concern was currently spending. The organisation protested but the local authority pointed out that what it was asking for was perfectly possible with the finance which it was willing to continue to provide. When Age Concern explained that the local authority's money had to be spread across all its activities, the local authority indicated that it was only interested in the day centres.

A local authority's resourcing and priorities may of course mean that it can only pay for specific services and not for all of what the voluntary organisation wishes to offer. Where this is the case, the local authority should be careful to recognise that it is right and appropriate for the voluntary organisation to maintain a wider role even if this has to be funded from other sources and that it has no wish or intention to prevent the voluntary group from doing anything else outside the contract which is legal and consistent with its mission. An issue which hopefully is now being resolved by local authorities is that of recognising that contracts should be offered not only in the narrow sense of supporting service provision to individuals but also in respect of services which a voluntary organisation may be providing to the wider community.

This includes services provided by Welfare Rights Groups, Advisory Services and local Development Agencies who support the voluntary sector in general. The Local Government Management Board has recently pointed to the danger of local authorities neglecting their community leadership role as they concentrate on service provision and internal management structures.

Campaigning

There is often a specific concern amongst voluntary organisations about their campaigning role. This is not necessarily a new concern related to contracting; voluntary organisations have always been uncertain about a statutory funders reactions to its campaigning, particularly if it is campaigning against the policies and priorities of its funder. Equally, many statutory bodies have questioned why they should be expected to fund a hand that seeks to slap them. This concern is probably sharpened in the contracting situation and it may be that some authorities have put 'no campaigning' clauses in their contracts although if this has happened, examples are not known to the author. On the other hand, where voluntary organisations in Oxfordshire have been particularly apprehensive that the contract would interfere with their right to campaign, their local authority has been willing to include a clause in the contract stating quite specifically that the organisations right to campaign is respected. This is subject only to the proviso that the voluntary organisation should not use the local authority's payments to engage in activities which the local authority is expressly forbidden to support by Part II of the 1986 Local Government

Act. This broadly states that the local authority should not publish material which will influence support for a political party and should not use its money to enable any other organisation to do so either.

Local authorities should not fear voluntary organisations which campaign. The culture which produces contracting as a mechanism and which embraces greater user choice and involvement in service provision as a goal should welcome organisations which support users in participating in the process of defining their needs and in monitoring how effectively these are being addressed by statutory bodies. Again in Oxfordshire the authority has been pleased to fund groups such as the Oxfordshire Council for Disabled people which have been established specifically to mobilise disabled people to represent themselves and campaign on their behalf for better services. The funding has been provided through a service agreement which actually requires that they should be effective in this role.

Management Skills

Voluntary organisations will be aware that to successfully negotiate and manage a contract, they will need to have explicit management skills. Often, organisations have been used to managing on a wing and a prayer and usually getting by but this is an unplanned approach to management and a contract demands a planned approach. Organisations need to be able to assess accurately their financial needs during the period that a contract is likely to run and to demonstrate that they have the ability to provide the service contracted to them. For the larger voluntary organisations, this may not be a big problem but for smaller ones who rely heavily on an input from volunteers then this will be more problematic. Local authorities should therefore be careful to compensate for these weaknesses and build into their contract management facilities for supplementing skills which the voluntary organisation may lack.

This may well imply working at "both ends of the contract" but the benefits are likely to be considerable both in output terms and in terms of good will for the partnership which will be generated. In supplementing the management skills of a voluntary organisation however, the local authority must be careful not to blur what should be clear responsibilities. The voluntary organisation will only grow in stature, confidence and management ability if it realises its own ultimate responsibility for delivering the service as contracted.

In one authority, responsibility for running a craft group was given to the local Society for the Blind. The group asked for and received support from the local authority for employing a member of staff and hiring a room. When, at the time of review, it was noticed that the voluntary organisation had not taken out adequate insurance policies, it became apparent that the group had not fully appreciated that they were expected to take ultimate management responsibility for the activity. They had rather assumed that the relationship was that they were providing volunteers for an activity managed by the Social Services Department.

Legal Liabilities

The Trustees of many voluntary organisations do not sufficiently well understand their responsibilities in law for the management of the organisation. Contracting tends to make them more aware and it is sometimes helpful to enable them to develop a sense of perspective. A contract should never expect more of a voluntary organisation than they can realistically be expected to deliver and local authorities should be extremely careful about seeking to impose penalty clauses which may be a source of considerable anxiety to the Trustees of the voluntary organisation and of doubtful utility, even if things do go wrong. Voluntary organisations often do not have much in the way of reserves and if they are local groups, there is probably a strong contrary indication to taking them to law if things do in fact go wrong. It is much better therefore that contracts should be non-threatening and that there are ample opportunities for a contract to be terminated relatively painlessly if the voluntary organisation is unable to fulfil it or if the local authority has strong grounds for arguing that the organisation is in breach of the conditions for carrying it through. In practical terms, this will probably mean that a local authority will seek no more that to recover any unspent monies transferred if a service is not delivered as agreed.

In one local authority where responsibility for running day care was to be transferred to Age Concern, the local authority lawyers were anxious to include a clause in the contract which stated that Age Concern were responsible at all times for the service and that if for any reason they failed to deliver it during the contract period the local authority could make alternative arrangements at Age Concern's expense. The proposed contract did not make allowances for unforeseen circumstances such as the roof blowing off which would certainly curtail the service and since Age Concern had little by way of reserves, would leave them powerless to provide the service at all.

In another local authority the contract simply said that if for any reason Age Concern were unable to deliver the service, the local authority could terminate the contract and would be entitled to the return of any grant proportionate to the period of time for which the service had not been provided. In the first situation the Age Concern group felt disabled and fearful of going ahead with the contract. In the second example, the group felt facilitated and positive.

Costs

Negotiating contracts is time consuming and time is money. If a voluntary organisation has to call in legal and accountancy expertise, then these will be additional costs that have to be borne.

This is a major source of concern for organisations which traditionally and admirably seek to operate with minimal overheads. Local authorities should recognise this and seek through the contract to compensate the voluntary organisation for any additional costs which arise from the contracting process. The conditions which local authorities may ask the voluntary organisation to comply with are also likely to increase the costs of the organisation in carrying out the activity and it should be recognised as reasonable that these should be borne by the local authority.

One contract with a neighbourhood centre included a requirement that the organisation should take into account the needs of disabled people. They wished to use two disabled people as volunteers in their advice service but the potential volunteers needed help with transport. The local authority were asked and agreed to meet the cost of this transport.

Ideology

When a local authority seeks to introduce contracting, some voluntary groups may automatically associate this with contracting out of Local Government services. If they have strong political views about this, they may be resistant to signing a contract. It is of course for the local authority to decide what are its intentions in introducing contracting. It may indeed be part of a much wider policy of contracting out services generally but experience so far indicates that few local authorities are going to this extreme. Therefore, in order to secure the benefits which contracts can provide in terms of bringing clarity and accountability into a relationship, a local authority should be specific and honest about its wider intentions. If voluntary organisations can see that they are not contributing to the wholesale dismemberment of a local authority's provider functions, they may be less resistant.

If there is such resistance then there is very little that a local authority can do about it except perhaps to continue to offer grant aid on an annual basis. They will presumably feel inclined to seek this solution if the service being offered by the voluntary organisation is one which can not be provided in any other way. If on the other hand there are alternative providers in the voluntary or the private sector, the local authority will go to them in the interests of longer term stability and the voluntary organisation will have to live with the consequences.

Competition in the Voluntary Sector

There is concern that through the development of contracting voluntary organisations will be forced to compete with each other for contracts from the local authority. Each local authority will have to assess for itself how realistic these sorts of fears are likely to be and of course the system for choosing voluntary organisations to contract with will have a considerable bearing on the answer.

Since there is little evidence that local authorities are seeking to put the kinds of services which voluntary organisations are best fitted to provide out to competitive tender, it may be that the fears of voluntary organisations are not particularly well founded. If, on the other hand, local authorities started giving contracts to national voluntary organisations to provide services which hitherto had been provided by local voluntary organisations through grant aid, then local groups might have substantial cause for concern.

User Involvement

The Contract Culture is supposed to be about empowering the user. Unfortunately, as yet, an understanding of how this can be achieved is not very well developed. Indeed, it is arguable that consumerism in its wider sense in the UK is not very well developed. Particular problems for local authorities are that they have to deal with conflicting perceptions about who represents the users interest. Many voluntary organisations believe that they represent the user interest yet local authorities may reasonably take the view that they must look wider even than this. On the other hand, elected members may take the view that they represent the user and often they do not take kindly to being told that even they may not have an overriding claim. Direct client surveys and monitoring of complaints procedures are likely to be used increasingly as mechanisms to ascertain what users really want and these are mechanisms which should be incorporated by voluntary organisations into their own management systems.

The crucial point at which users need to be involved is that of drawing up the service specification. It is users needs which specifications are intended to address and unless they can have some influence at that point, user involvement will be mere lip service. On the other hand, user choice will be limited by available resources which is necessarily one of the great conflicts in the Community Care legislation. What is the value of full assessment of need if there is not a comprehensive provision to respond?

Picking a way through this minefield is a major challenge to voluntary organisations. In the past they have perhaps simplistically been able to argue that their services are a direct response to identified need.

The grants culture colluded with this to a large extent, seeming to imply by local authorities giving grants that this was indeed the case. In future, voluntary organisations will have to demonstrate that their services are not simply their own interpretation of what users want but are in fact services which users have chosen on the basis of preference and towards whose development they contribute.

Charging Policy

Voluntary agencies have largely determined their own

attitude towards charging for their services. This has been influenced mainly by the amount of income which they need to balance the books. Most voluntary organisations recognise that volunteers are not willing to give time and energies freely to activities for which the recipient is expected to make a substantial payment. Local authorities contracting with voluntary organisations are likely to have their own view about what it is reasonable to charge the recipient of a service however and the amount that they are prepared to pay is likely to reflect their expectations of what it is reasonable to expect a user to contribute. Voluntary organisations are therefore concerned that local authorities will influence their own charging policies which could lead to the alienation of voluntary support. This in turn will increase the cost of the service to both the voluntary organisation and the local authority and if the local authority is not prepared to pay what the voluntary organisation reckons is necessary to maintain a service of a standard acceptable to the voluntary organisation, then the voluntary organisation clearly will have severe difficulties.

Summary

It will be clear that voluntary organisations will have many anxieties about the effect of the contracting process and that local authorities wishing to use the voluntary sector as contractors must try to understand the voluntary sector perspective. This implies consultation on a fairly extensive scale in order that local authorities can identify for themselves what the primary concerns of voluntary organisations in their own area are and how these might be addressed.

Chapter 4
The Challenge of Contracting and Local Authorities

If contracting forces voluntary organisations to re-think the way they organise themselves and the way they relate to local authorities, it poses a challenge of equal magnitude to local authorities themselves. Giving grant aid, even in the traditional way, was not always a well thought out process for local authorities, nor did it necessarily indicate a significant commitment to the voluntary sector.

Political Perspectives

There are no well defined party political perspectives on grant aiding voluntary groups. Conservatives can easily be found who will argue that voluntary organisations should do as much as possible because the state should only intervene where people can not find their own solutions to problems. On the other hand, they will have colleagues who, whilst agreeing with the principle, will extend it with an argument that the state should not finance voluntary organisations since their activities should be entirely self funded or funded through private and corporate beneficence.

Labour Party supporters on the other hand may be found

who would want to make significant provision for grant aid to encourage community participation whilst others would not believe in giving financial support to voluntary organisations on the grounds that democratically elected authorities should be directly providing any services which the community needs.

The Grants Process

Each local authority has therefore tended to develop its own personality in relation to the voluntary sector.

Some local authorities budget for considerable provision of grant aid as part of a package of support to the community and voluntary sector which includes provision of buildings, transport, training and staff support through community development workers. At the other extreme, local authorities can be found with tiny grants budgets distributed at the whim of their members. In between is a range which includes voluntary organisations being used as service providers which are more or less tied in to services provided by local authorities.

The actual process by which decisions in relation to grant aid are made also vary considerably from authority to authority. In some, detailed applications have to be submitted which are scrutinised by officers who make reports to members in committee. Such authorities may have well developed policies to govern their priorities and the grant making process may fall into some logical framework. In other authorities, there may be no well defined policy for grant aid and judgements are made on the basis of submissions by voluntary organisations which are taken at face value or which rely heavily on the personal experiences of members and anecdotal evidence from "the patch". Where there is a strong member involvement in the grant making process, this may in fact result in a tactical withdrawal by officers from the process. It would not be unusual to find officers who believe that grant aid to voluntary organisations is such a peripheral part of the activities of their authority that it is not worth their jeopardising their own standing and careers by commenting or contributing to a process which can often be quite controversial. This is likely to be the case especially in those areas where voluntary organisations have learnt or been taught that success in the grants ballot is dependent upon their ability to successfully lobby for their cause.

The Contract Process

If the world of grant aid was and is as loose and as random as described, it is hardly surprising that pressure is being put on local authorities to approach grant aid in a more systematic and rational manner. Deciding to offer support through contracts inevitably means that a process of rationalisation has begun. It means that a local authority will have to think clearly about who it gives money to and why. It means that its relationships with those who are supported, those in other words who get contracts, will be more formalised. This in turn means that a local authority is likely to become more formalised in its relationship with the voluntary sector as a whole.

The structure which a local authority uses for relating to the voluntary sector through contracting does not have to be the same as that which it uses for its other contractual relationships. In fact, if it is wise, it will think afresh since the process which, for example has developed to deal with organisations providing services for profit, is not likely to be helpful when dealing with a voluntary organisation to run a family centre. Some authorities appear not to have seen this distinction, and it is then not surprising that the voluntary sector complains that it can make no sense of what is happening. They have therefore alienated a sector which has potentially an enormous amount to offer as partners in servicing the needs of the local community. This is particularly true of social services departments where an impetus to develop contracting has been given by the Community Care legislation.

One likely and indeed desirable effect of contracting is that the services which voluntary organisations provide can be brought into the mainstream of local authority provision. In other words, the services which the voluntary organisation delivers can be evaluated alongside those delivered by the local authority itself or even those provided through the private sector. The grant approach, even when it was substantial and worthwhile, often failed to bring voluntary and local authority practices together. Dealing with voluntary organisations was often seen as a specialism in its own right and one which took precedence over issues of managing particular kinds of service.

Some local authorities have sections dealing with grants and sometimes these are centrally based, other times they are departmentally based. In either case, they are separate and distinct from service delivery operations. Hence, for example, whilst local authority day centres are supported by the management resources of the authority, the voluntary sector day centre may not be given any local authority support at all other than the cash that is transferred. If there is a supportive liaison relationship, it is likely to be with someone who is not a specialist in providing care but rather a specialist in supporting voluntary organisations. These were problems which could be overcome, but quite often they were ignored.

Purchaser/Provider – The Split

Contracting therefore forces local authorities to identify how the client/contractor split is to be handled. In turn this will vary depending upon the structure which the local authority has opted to adopt.

Those authorities which have adopted a radical split between purchasers and contractors will probably decide that contracts with the voluntary sector should be managed by their purchaser function. This means that a process will be developed in that function for:

1. Auditing the ability of a voluntary organisation to provide a service at all

2. Systems for differentiating between organisations if there is a choice of prospective contractors

3. Drafting specifications

4. Drawing up contracts

5. Managing them.

Even if the local authority does not organise itself quite so radically, it still needs to work out how the contracting processes will work, and what is arranged is of crucial importance to the voluntary sector.

Useful lessons for managing this process have been available to local authorities from their experiences of compulsory competitive tendering where staff involved in cleaning and catering services for example had to be separated into client side and contractor side. Expertise which was really needed in both areas had to be separated and reallocated to one side or the other. There was a commensurate danger that both sides ended up being the poorer because expertise had been dissipated.

Contracts and Community Development

Local authorities must be aware that as they try to develop their own technical competence for auditing and assessing suppliers, drawing up contracts and managing them, it is vital to build in an understanding and respect for the values which are the strengths of voluntary organisations. It should therefore adopt an approach to contracting which draws on community development skills and encourage these in the purchasing function. This is entirely consistent with responsibilities which new legislation has placed on local authorities to support, encourage and develop the external market place. The danger is that if this emphasis is not built into the purchaser side, it will be lost altogether since an inevitable consequence of departments splitting purchaser/provider is that those in-house and external agencies which are the providers are likely to view each other competitively. Thus the local authority day centre which previously may have offered informal support and assistance to the neighbouring voluntary day centre may, in a contracting environment, be much less likely to provide such advice and support. In this sense, contracting has made a difference; the culture gradually becomes one of competitiveness where knowledge, expertise and experience become tradable commodities. It is unfortunate but it is a fact.

Most local authorities as yet do not appear to have chosen the radical option of splitting themselves into purchaser and contractor units. They still have the same issues to deal with but the solutions may be less clear cut. We can look at some of these issues.

1. Assessment of Potential Suppliers

Any contracting process has to begin with a process of assessing the suitability of a potential supplier. There is no point in spending time trying to negotiate a contract with an organisation who is not at the beginning seen as capable of delivering the service required or suitable to do it. Where organisations have previously received grant aid, then they may be "deemed" to be suitable, but when a local authority seeks to develop new services, it will need some appropriate mechanisms for making assessments. This assessment is likely to be a comprehensive enquiry and analysis into an organisations credentials for providing care.

What Will It Look At?

The assessment will consider an organisations:

* Management structure
* Financial stability

* Its track record
* Its values
* Its relationship with other providers

It should enable the local authority to answer with confidence the question "is this an organisation we can trust to provide care to vulnerable people?". Local authorities clearly need to decide who carries out this process. Some of the elements involved include financial expertise and professional expertise in the particular service to be provided. It may also however be necessary to involve health and safety experts and specialists in personnel issues.

It may well be that the local authority will have to leave the co-ordination of the assessment of potential suppliers with an officer who may also have responsibilities as a manager of directly provided services. The one role could complement the other but clearly there may be conflicts involved as well, if a potential supplier from outside is likely to be in competition with the in-house provider.

2. Choosing a Supplier

There are various options for choosing a supplier, they include:

* Competitive tendering – scarcely any authorities have done this so far.

* Negotiate with a number of potential suppliers - this is a common practice, particularly when the local authority wants to test out what might be on offer at what price.

* Negotiate with a single preferred supplier - a common way for local authorities to do business since it often involves continuing to deal with someone who is known and trusted. Sometimes known as "Sweetheart Deals".

* Create a new supplier - this involves setting up a new organisation. Occasionally this can involve hiving off part

of the local authority's own activities but more usually it involves working with a new community group.

There are clearly advantages and disadvantages in each.

Competitive Tendering

Advantages of completely open competitive tendering are that a potential supplier may be identified who has previously been unknown, and that the lowest cost provider will be identified.

A disadvantage, if the competition is truly open, is that the supplier will not have been previously assessed. The process for choosing a supplier from those who have submitted tenders must therefore allow for time to be spent in carrying out an auditing process which can be time consuming. It is argued that competitive tendering provides the most level of playing fields and may lead to the best price being obtained. However the cost of the process both to the local authority who is seeking tenders and to organisations which may be bidding for them must be taken into account. In this context it is important to remember that many voluntary organisations may not feel it to be financially worthwhile the risk of entering into the field in this way.

Negotiating with a Number of Potential Suppliers

This may be the preferred option for local authorities that wish to deal with voluntary organisations and develop contractual relationships with them whilst at the same time being seen to make some attempt to create competition.

Negotiating with a Single Supplier

This is probably the nearest to the way relationships are likely to have been conducted in the past although it leaves a local authority open to the charge that it is practising nepotism. On the other hand, experience may have shown a local authority that the close relationship which can arise from this type of relationship allows it to see for itself in some detail that the organisation is offering a cost effective service.

Direct negotiation with organisations to find a supplier which avoids a tendering process allows for looser specifications to be drawn up at the onset, and it therefore allows for flexibility in approach and for opportunity to be given to the supplier influencing the eventual specification agreed as the basis for the contract.

Creating a New Organisation

This is likely to be an appropriate way of meeting needs where there is little confidence in existing potential suppliers or where the need to be addressed is unique and bringing together the expertise of a group of voluntary organisations or individuals is considered to be the best way of bringing this experience together.

Local authorities must decide their attitude towards choosing their suppliers and keep their options as open as their local political circumstances will allow. Which ever options are chosen, local authorities will have to demonstrate that they have good reasons for choosing the route concerned and that they are providing encouragement and opportunity for all potential suppliers to be involved in providing the services needed.

Decision making about the preferred mechanism for choosing suppliers should be made at the highest level of the department and clear guidance published for both the voluntary sector and for managers lower down in the local authority hierarchy.

Unless this happens, then there is a danger of mistrust

developing if some voluntary organisations feel that they are not being given due consideration or that some voluntary organisations are achieving preferred supplier status on grounds which are not understood or justified.

3. Drawing up the Specification

Producing a specification is the most crucial phase of the contracting process since it is the point where the service to be purchased is defined. It is therefore essential that there should be clarity about the kind and quality of service which is expected and to ensure at the earliest stage that what is written into the specification is what is needed to satisfy the needs being addressed.

It must primarily be the responsibility of the purchaser to take the lead on drawing up the specification but this should be done in conjunction with the end users and in appropriate cases, their carers. The purchasers should also recognise that the chosen supplier may wish to contribute useful input into the specification and allow for this. Voluntary organisations usually have high commitment to providing quality services and their experience as providers who are often closer to their public is an essential part of the added value which they may bring to a contract. Deciding who should be involved in drawing up specifications may however be quite a challenge for many local authorities since it implies new skills.

There may be a temptation to call upon expertise developed in compulsory competitive tendering but, as indicated before, this may be quite limiting. The services which have been subject to CCT are on the whole services which large commercial undertakings could be expected to bid for and the specifications had to be prepared in advance of the tendering process. Local authorities tended to err on the side of caution and produce highly specific specifications intended to tie bidders down. It is important that in developing an approach to the voluntary sector, local authorities identify people to draw up specifications who the voluntary sector can relate to. These will probably be professionals who can understand the values of the voluntary sector and their concerns to provider user friendly services whilst also recognising that they may need help and training in developing skills in relation to drafting on paper. This, in turn, begs the question of how to develop an approach to writing specifications and indeed contracts which are clear and as uncomplicated as possible.

4. Drafting the Contract

A major issue for many local authorities has been who drafts a contract. Often this is seen as a legal issue and one to be handled by solicitors. Handing the whole process over to lawyers is not only expensive, but also can lead to a way of looking at the task which can interfere with the objective of keeping it simple. Yet, where local authorities have tried to keep the contracts simple and perhaps used words such as grant agreement or service agreement, there has then been a doubt as to whether these are really contracts at all.

It is suggested here that any agreement accepted by the parties is a contract. If the object of the contract is to draw up a clear statement of expectation and commitments rather than to provide a basis for possible future legal action then that can be reflected in the actual document being as simple as the task allows. Local authorities must therefore recognise that lawyers are advisors, they will tend to play safe and they will tend to anticipate the worst. There is in fact likely to be a whole range of situations where contracts will be used but where it would be unrealistic to contemplate that even if they went wrong a local authority would be likely to resort to action in court.

Many contracts with voluntary organisations to provide social care for example, are likely to be relatively small and the organisation contracted to provide the service is likely to have little by way of reserves. The sensible approach for the local authority in these circumstances is to ensure that the sums of money transferred at any one time are merely sufficient to keep the service running and to recognise in the contract, explicitly and implicitly, that if things did go wrong, the local authority's claim would be limited to recovery of unspent monies transferred.

Clearly, if large sums of money are being transferred and if the commitment of the contract is over many years, and if the service is to be a main line statutory service, then a local authority would take a different view and would be concerned that there were arrangements for proper recompense to the local authority if the contract went wrong and had to be terminated.

What is probably needed therefore is a range of different types of contract from the simple to the more complicated and where non-legal officers can operate the more simple ones within a framework approved by the lawyers but drawn up by the officers who have to manage the contract. An example of a pro forma system for producing such agreements and used successfully in Oxfordshire is attached as Appendix 1. Other examples can be found in the Department of Health Guidance "Purchase of Service".

5. Negotiating the Contract

An issue for local authorities is who actually carries out the negotiations with voluntary organisations which lead to the drawing up of the contract. In those which already have the contract management facilities developed for the purposes of CCT, there may be a temptation to locate the function there. It should be clear from what has previously been written that this could be a mistake. Voluntary organisations who have experience of dealing with such local authorities have complained that they are dealing with a remote bureaucracy whose approach to contracting shows no understanding of the circumstances of voluntary organisations and that in consequence, voluntary organisations are not putting themselves forward as potential service providers. It seems better that local authority lead negotiators should be people who understand the services which are to be provided, probably because they have managed such services themselves, but that incorporated into the negotiating team are people who have expertise about contracts, finance and the management of voluntary organisations.

Thus the negotiators will go into the negotiations with a clear view of the needs to be addressed and a reasonable price to pay but will have the flexibility to accommodate the circumstances of the supplying organisations and an open mindedness to benefit from their expertise. This means that local authorities will need to have key managers as co-ordinators of the contracting process who have a general awareness of all these aspects but will involve a variety of other managers as appropriate in individual situations. In Oxfordshire, a Principal Officer with wide experience of liaising with the voluntary sector has been given the Key Co-ordinating role and has produced the checklist illustrated at appendix one in conjunction with the legal department yet the negotiations about specific contracts will be carried out by managers at third tier level who are responsible for service provision for the specific client groupings. The Treasurers Department checks draft agreements to ensure that the financial arrangements are appropriate and ultimately each agreement is signed by the Director.

In another authority, contracts are drawn up using a prepared format by Managers without any central overview up to a limit of a few thousand pounds after which time the process becomes more complicated and involves more managers and the involvement of the authority's legal department. There are therefore different ways of deciding who should handle the negotiations and this is an issue which local authorities will have to decide for themselves provided they are clear what they are trying to achieve and fully recognise that there needs to be different skill inputs into the process.

Also that the people carrying out the negotiations need training and support, the permutations for actually carrying out the process are fairly numerous.

6. Contract Management

Once a contract is in place, someone within the local authority must take responsibility for managing it. Often, the function will be located with those who took the lead in the negotiations. Managing the contract will involve:

* Ascertaining that the conditions of the contract are being complied with

* Maintaining effective liaison between the organisation providing the service, the organisation paying for it and users

* Ensuring that there is a mechanism for mutual notification and acknowledgement of difficulties

* Having known means for taking prompt action to address difficulties.

Contract management is a task to be taken seriously and adequate time and training must be made available to those asked to undertake such tasks. In an authority that does not have a separate purchaser unit, it is likely that the contract management role will be undertaken by a manager who has responsibility for providing a service to the client group who the contractor is employed to serve.

Some authorities however which do not have a radical purchaser/provider split have nevertheless appointed a separate cadre of contract monitors for voluntary organisations.

These monitors are not involved very much in negotiating the initial agreement and are people with a community development background who have been redeployed into this new role. They do therefore have expertise at relating to the voluntary sector. Time will tell whether this is an effective way of handling the contract management role. It certainly means that it is being given appropriate significance but it suffers from the disadvantage that the contract management role is being treated as being separate from that of choosing the suppliers and negotiating contracts yet this earlier stage can provide a valuable opportunity for preparing the way for effective contract management later.

These are a fairly formidable series of issues for local authorities to address but unless they are carefully thought through, the local authority is likely to present a picture of confusion to individual voluntary organisations who may wish to have a contractual relationship with it. At this stage of evolution, it is clear that some authorities have not distinguished these issues. Some that have, tried to develop a systematic approach to resolving them, usually by setting up departmental working parties to think through the issues in order that policy and practice can be evolved.

Chapter 5
Specifying the Service to be Provided

This and the next three chapters will look at the detail of contracts. In looking at the detail of what must go into contracts, it should not be assumed that the important issue is simply to get a contract written. All High Street shops produce contracts to be used if a purchase is to be affected through a deferred payment agreement but hardly anyone reads them and the process of signing them therefore achieves very little in terms of developing a relationship between purchaser and seller. It is hardly surprising therefore that when things go wrong, they usually go wrong fairly badly, leading to a rapid breakdown of trust and ready recourse to litigation or the threat of it.

Contracts Should Have Meaning

Contracts between local authorities and voluntary organisations should have meaning and the process of drawing them up should be allowed time to develop. There has been criticism from many students of contracting expressed at a number of national conferences, that it often takes six months or more for a local authority and a voluntary organisation to negotiate a contract. This criticism may be misplaced. Contracts for care are important documents, they define a service and a relationship between purchaser and supplier. If, as a result of a protracted negotiating process, a greater understanding of what supplier and purchaser each has to offer the other has been achieved, the time has been well spent. As we have previously indicated, when it is possible for the specification to be drawn up in consultation with the prospective voluntary organisation supplying, this is likely to be the most important part of the process. It is when clarification about the service to be offered and the standards to which it can be provided will take place and this will be the focus later for the monitoring process.

A number of local authorities, including Oxfordshire, Wiltshire and Birmingham, have developed a checklist for drawing up specifications which address the issues involved and this has been found helpful in a number of ways.

Firstly, it is helpful to the voluntary organisation if it is made available in advance because they are able to focus on the issues on the local authority's agenda. It is in fact helpful if they are encouraged to use the checklist to prepare their own draft specification in advance of any meeting with the local authority to discuss the contract.

Secondly, it is helpful to the local authority's own negotiators since unless an authority has made a fairly radical purchaser/ contractor split, those involved in taking the lead and negotiating contracts with the voluntary sector are likely to be service managers who have busy lives and for whom negotiating contracts is but a small part of their total workload. A checklist therefore ensures that both the voluntary organisation and the local authority's own staff start at the same point.

Thirdly, a checklist which is widely recognised and commonly used is a reassurance to the voluntary sector as a whole that the local authority is treating it evenhandedly. As a corollary of this, it might be useful for voluntary sector organisations to equip themselves with their own corresponding checklists to ensure that all their interests are covered.

Much has already been written in the Department of Health Guidance on the subject of how a service specification should be drawn up and what issues should be addressed but a simple checklist may include the following:

1. What is to be provided?

A specification must address the issue of what is to be provided, whether this be simple or complex. It may be useful therefore to look first at a broad description and then break this down into specifics and finally detail. For example, a specification for a Day Centre might begin by saying that the service to be provided is day care for elderly people but then go on to indicate whether it is for all elderly people or simply some categories of elderly people, mentally infirm elderly people with incontinence problems perhaps.

The specification may then continue by describing the specific items of service which will be on offer which could include facilities for taking a bath, hairdressing, chiropody, fitness activities, recreation and the taking of a midday meal. Contracts can of course be used for innovative purposes and for a developmental project what is to be provided might describe a research or investigatory process leading to the identification of needs and indicating some choices about how they might be met.

2. What can be said about service standards?

This question should prompt consideration of the standards which will be expected or aimed for.

If the voluntary organisation has a code of practice, the specification may simply indicate that the organisation will operate in accordance with it, but for organisations that do not have such documentation, the question may usefully focus minds on what really is to happen and an attempt should be made to get behind the rhetoric. Simply referring to a quality service is not good enough. Specification should define what a quality service is. On the other hand, avoid wherever possible, getting tangled up in minutiae. Perhaps a requirement for 'a nourishing meal which takes account of individual needs' is a better way of describing the luncheon service than to attempt to define the proportions of fat, fibre and carbohydrates in the meal, its calorific value and the temperature at which it must be served, not withstanding that these factors are themselves important.

3. Who is eligible to receive the service?

There is a need to clarify who can receive a service whilst making clear that there are no unfair restrictions.

Some services will be restricted to certain age groups or people from particular localities or to people with particular kinds of disabilities or needs. This needs to be agreed and included in the contract since it is easy for there to be a drift away from original objectives, particularly for voluntary organisations subject to community pressures and where there may be a tendency for open access.

4. How is access to be obtained?

The question of access to services is important. Do referrals have to come through the Social Services department, the Health Authority, other professionals or is it at the discretion of the voluntary organisation itself. There is also a need to deal with issues about the use of vacant spaces and about the arrangements which will be made to publicise the availability of the service in order that those who do have rights of access are aware of the facility and the terms on which it is available.

5. How much of the service will be provided?

It is essential to address issues of quantity, availability and regularity. Thus there should be a clear agreement about how often the service is to be provided in terms of the number of weeks in the year, days in the week, hours in the day, that a service will be open. Also, how much of it will be provided; this could be in terms of how many meals will be served, how many people will be accommodated at a day centre, how many volunteers will be recruited, trained, supported. What will be the capacity of a family centre or the number of hours of domiciliary care that will be given for the payment to be received?

These are sometimes issues which it is painful to address, particularly if a voluntary organisation has a history of "doing its best". Part of the discipline of the contract culture is that everybody must be more specific about what they are going to do in order that users can have a clear understanding of what is available to them.

Voluntary organisations, as with any other contractors, will need to make commitments about how much they are committed to achieve.

No doubt local authorities and voluntary organisations will wish to develop their own checklists which will add to the above list but if there is a clear understanding of what is to be provided, to what standards with eligibility and accessibility clear, then a reasonable start will have been made.

6. Open or Closed Specifications?

The way that specifications are framed will have to take account of course of whether a finite service is needed or whether scope is wanted in the specification for the service to develop and change. Open specifications are more developmental in their approach and are particularly suitable where the purchaser wishes to encourage the contractor to innovate, experiment, extend and develop. One specification for a family centre for example stated that the Management

Committee would consult families with young children in their locality where the family centre was situated and evolve with them programmes and projects for the benefit of parents and their children. A service agreement with a Council for Voluntary Service said that the organisation would identify and promote new opportunities for voluntary involvement and provide support to emerging organisations and groups during their stages of formation and then provide ongoing training and co-ordination.

These sort of agreements contrast with situations where the local authority as a purchaser has a very clear understanding of precisely what it needs from a contractor in terms of output. A voluntary organisation providing domiciliary care for example would be likely to find that the number of hours required would be tightly drawn up and there would be a careful definition of what service was to be provided for users during those hours. A relatively small contract with a voluntary organisation providing day care is equally explicit. It states:

a. The Committee will provide a day centre for the benefit of people who are elderly or disabled which shall include the provision of a meal, comfort and support to users and opportunities for recreational and social activities.

b. The Committee will develop friendship between users of the day centre and follow up, in their own homes or in hospital, people who through illness are unable to attend in person.

c. Offer advice and practical support.

d. Provide transport where necessary to enable users to reach the day centre.

e. The day centre will be open at least between the hours of 10am until 2pm one day per week for approximately fifty weeks of the year and will cater for fifty people from the Carebury area.

The tighter that a specification in an agreement is drawn up, the more likely it is that any changes would need to be negotiated in the context of a review of the agreement.

7. User and Carer Involvement

The involvement of users and carers in drawing up specifications for services is a vital link in the chain of meeting the Governments objectives for community care as outlined in "Caring for People; community care in the next decade and beyond". This places particular importance on the need for services to be responsive to the needs and choices of users and to take into account the separate needs of carers. The Government's key components for community care are defined as:

* Services that respond flexibly and sensitively to the needs of individuals and their carers.
* Services that allow a range of options for consumers.
* Services that intervene no more than is necessary to foster independence.
* Services that concentrate on those with greatest needs.

Whilst it may not always be practicable to involve users or carers in the direct negotiations with voluntary organisations about a contract, there are many opportunities to consult with both of these groups about their service needs. Specifications in draft form can always be sent to user or carer groups for comment. Another approach to this issue which is being developed in Oxfordshire is for model specifications for different kinds of services to be developed in forums where users and carers are represented and which are then passed to the negotiators for consideration when an individual contract is being drawn up.

Notwithstanding the input which is made by users and carers into the initial process of producing specifications, agreements should always provide for review and as we shall discuss later, users and carers should always have access to the review process.

8. Quality versus Price

It is sometimes said, probably most unfairly, that in any contract the objective of the contractor is to obtain the highest price for the lowest quality and for the purchaser to obtain the highest quality for the lowest price.

In negotiation involving a voluntary organisation however a local authority can reasonably expect that the objectives of both the local authority and the voluntary organisation are similar - "to produce the best possible service for the most economical price". The specification will identify what the quality of the service is to be. It can not therefore be finalised without reference to the price which the local authority is able and prepared to pay. Local authorities have finite resources, voluntary organisations sometimes have a means of adding value; the process of deciding the quality price issue may therefore be more complex than could be the case in a straight forward deal with a commercial undertaking.

In discussing a specification with a voluntary organisation there is therefore a need for honesty by both parties about where they stand. A local authority should indicate the minimum standard it will accept and what standards it would aspire to achieving.

The voluntary organisation must be equally realistic. Given current financial circumstances, a local authority may only be able to pay for a service which matches its minimum quality standards; it is honest and realistic if that, then is the standard used in the contract specification. If the voluntary organisation is able to exceed that standard, it should be recognised that this is value which the voluntary organisation is adding to the contract gratuitously and is not a service enhancement which is being paid for by the local authority. It would be silly to agree a specification which the voluntary organisation might not be able to sustain if its own circumstances changed.

A real dilemma emerges of course if the voluntary

organisations definition of an acceptable standard exceeds that of the local authority's and particularly that which the local authority is able to pay for. There is then an impasse.

Chapter 6
Requirements on the Voluntary Organisation as a Contractor

One of the difficulties of talking about the voluntary sector is that it is so diverse. The voluntary sector encompasses huge national organisations on the one hand whose Chief Executives match the status and salaries of their counterparts in local authorities and on the other, it encompasses small community groups who work entirely on the basis of voluntary effort. In developing contracting relationships, particularly in seeking partners to provide caring services, local authorities may be dealing with the whole spectrum. Whilst hopefully local authorities' practices will recognise and provide for these differences, there will be basic minimal requirements of voluntary organisations at whatever level and these are what we shall discuss in this chapter.

What are Voluntary Organisations?

Representatives of voluntary organisations seeking a contract must first and foremost know who and what they are. Are they representing an incorporated or an unincorporated organisation? Are they the local branch of a national organisation or the Executive Committee of a local organisation? Are they a sub-group of the Executive

Committee, a subsidiary of the organisation, or are they even an unrepresentative splinter group acting in the name of the organisation? It may seem strange to labour this point but it is not unusual for members of voluntary organisations to be unclear about these matters. Yet contracts must be regarded as legal documents which incur responsibilities and the local authority must know who it is dealing with and whether the group of people who it is talking to are able to make commitments and if so, on whose behalf?

Just as local authorities have to clarify their policies and practices towards contracting and decide who they will authorise to act on their behalf and how they will deal with the process of negotiating and committing themselves to a contract, voluntary organisations must do likewise. What about the size of contracts for example? Agreements have been struck with mainly national voluntary organisations or their branches for services costing many tens of thousands of pounds and with local community groups for services worth maybe only a few hundred pounds. Is it worth drawing up a contract for a few hundred pounds? This is an issue which voluntary organisations must decide and consult with their local authorities about. The process of drawing up a contract is time consuming but if we recall that the benefit of a contract is to bring clarity about expectations into a relationship and to set standards in the interests of satisfying the needs and protecting the user, then small contracts may be as important as big ones. It is as important for the elderly person who visits a luncheon club just one day a month as for another who visits a day centre every day that the organisations responsible for providing them with their services are committed to doing so in a way which ensures that the quality of the service offered is acceptable. A written agreement or contract should help to do that. Furthermore, if local authorities are encouraged by voluntary organisations only to think in terms of large contracts, it may be more difficult for local organisations to obtain them. Parting with large sums of money frightens local authorities, it may be in their interests and in the interests of voluntary groups that they be encouraged to go for smaller ones which may appear less daunting; perhaps even a number of separate, small contracts for the same organisation.

Distinctions within the Voluntary Sector

Important distinctions when considering voluntary organisations are their legal status and their areas of benefit.

Unincorporated Organisations

Most local voluntary organisations are unincorporated. In an unincorporated organisation ultimate responsibility for the management of the organisation is carried out by the Executive Committee members who are also the Trustees of the organisation (though they may not always be aware of this). If liabilities are incurred which the organisation cannot meet, then they fall on the Trustees who, in some circumstances, will be expected to meet any debts from their personal wealth.

Unincorporated voluntary organisations should therefore be particularly careful that they have proper systems for entering into contracts and that those who ultimately carry the responsibility know what risks they are being exposed to. There have been examples of members of a voluntary organisation being willing to enter into a contract with a local authority without the committee members being fully aware that this was happening in their name and that they would ultimately be expected to carry responsibility. Part of the difficulty is that many people good naturedly agree to become committee members of voluntary organisations without realising the responsibilities which they incur. Voluntary organisations considering entering into a contract should therefore make sure that members are aware of what they are doing and local authorities considering offering contracts to voluntary organisations should ensure that this awareness exists.

Incorporated Organisations

With an incorporated organisation, typically a charity that is also a Company Limited by Guarantee, the organisation itself is a legal entity and can enter into a contract in its own right. Trustees, committee members or the Board of Directors therefore enjoy some degree of protection; they are generally speaking limited to a contribution of £1 should the organisation go into liquidation. Committee members of an incorporated organisation do however have responsibilities as Company Directors and this includes a responsibility for playing a full part in the management of the organisation and ensuring that it is well managed. This again is a personal responsibility and not one which can be avoided. The ultimate responsibilities of Committee members of incorporated organisations may not therefore be too different from those of unincorporated ones, though they are better protected if things go wrong in spite of their having been involved actively and in good faith.

National Organisations

National voluntary organisations have differing policies about expansion and about contracting. Some are clearly interested in both, even to the extent that several have set up contracting departments. National voluntary organisations often have a strong appeal for local authorities since their structures can sometimes match that of the local authority itself. There may therefore be a feeling that a local authority is talking to a like minded being. National voluntary organisations may well have their own support structures to back up the contracting process and this can give them a ready appeal as prospective contractors for the local authority. In assessing national organisations as a provider of a service however, local authorities are likely to consider how well integrated the national organisation is in the local community.

If part of the advantage of working with voluntary organisations is that they bring a local community dimension, then it will be important to establish that they have one. If they don't, and some national voluntary organisations have parachuted into local areas to offer services, there is a danger that they will be resented by more truly local organisations and this could be to the detriment of the service which the local authority is seeking to procure.

Local Voluntary Organisations

It would be tragic if local voluntary organisations were frozen out of service provision because they were not seen to be capable of entering into contracts with the local authority. Where they rely heavily on a voluntary management committee and the use of volunteers for providing their services, they may have some realistic fears, and be reluctant to enter into the process. This is understandable, particularly in the light of the comments which we have made about the responsibilities of the trustees. Yet, local voluntary organisations may be particularly well equipped to provide services because they have roots in the local community, understand its needs and are able to mobilise help in an acceptable way. Whilst pressing local authorities to deal with them in a supportive and enabling way, they should also seek to help themselves. This will include trying to reinforce their management committees with the kind of expertise and skill which would be useful in contracting and would include legal, financial and negotiating skills.

Furthermore, they should seek opportunities for training themselves and their staff. The local authority can be asked to help with this process either by providing training direct or by providing grants to enable to local groups to buy it in.

Local groups should also rally round their Council for Voluntary Service or equivalent and ask for it to be enabled to offer support for the voluntary sector in contracting. If they have not already done so, such local development agencies should be negotiating their own contracts with the local authority for financial support to enable them to provide training and backup to the local voluntary sector in order that they may enter into contracts and meet the standards which will be implied.

Local Development Agencies

There is vital role for local development agencies in areas where contracting is being developed. Training has already been mentioned. They also need to be advocates on behalf of those voluntary groups who are worried about contracting. Local authorities should be dealing sympathetically with organisations who have previously offered services but have become unsure about the implications of entering into a contractual relationship. They should also be finding ways of dealing with small service providing groups if they have decided that there is a lower financial cut off point for contracts which the group falls below and they should also be considering how they continue to support those groups whose principal activities are advocacy or campaigning work. There is no reasons why these latter groups should not be offered contracts. If this is not considered appropriate then grant aid should be continued.

Grant Aid

There is a clear need for grants to continue in all authorities but there is a tendency in some that have gone down the contracting route to feel that they are now obsolete.

The local voluntary sector must make it clear that if they do not continue to receive priming grants then new initiatives will be stifled and the next generation of contractors will not emerge. They also need to make the point that advocacy is an essential part of consumerism and that if contracting is about developing a better responsiveness to user needs and choice then advocacy groups are helping the users to articulate these needs and choices. Finally, campaigning work not only supports advocacy but is also the means by which local people let their politicians know what is needed. The campaigning of voluntary groups can often create a climate where politicians can obtain or release funds and campaigning can therefore enhance and support the political process.

Specific Requirements on Voluntary Organisations

Local authorities are likely to seek specific undertakings from voluntary organisations when they are considering offering them a contract. These assurances may be sought at the auditing and assessment stage or more likely, they may be included as requirements in the contract itself. An obvious prerequisite is that the local authority will seek assurances that the voluntary organisation is able to manage itself appropriately in line with acceptable standards of management practice to achieve the ends described in the specification. We shall look at some of these aspects in terms of clauses which a local authority could ask to be included in an agreement.

Operational Policies

● "Voluntary organisations will respect the operational policies of the Social Services Department (this may be attached as an appendix to this agreement) and will take them into account at all times whilst discharging obligations under this agreement."

Working Practices

● "The voluntary organisation will provide a safe system of work for people working for it both paid and volunteer staff and for those using its facilities and shall have regard to the needs of disabled people."

A local authority will want to ensure that a voluntary organisation's working practices are satisfactory from Health and Safety perspectives and that their systems for working do not put those who work for them at risk. The reasons for this will be obvious. Not only do local authorities have a moral obligation to ensure that decent standards apply in all those areas which they have a capacity to influence but they will be mindful of various scandals which have occurred and where there has been justified criticism of the managing organisation.

A drugs counselling service for example would be foolish to have a working system which meant that individuals were left alone in a building that was open to the public. Organisations providing volunteers to escort young babies would be foolish if they did not ensure that there were adequate child seats in any vehicles to be used and would preferably ensure that there was an escort.

Local authorities will equally wish to ensure that working practices have regard to the needs of disabled people, both in terms of their rights to work for voluntary organisations as employees or volunteers and also to have access as users.

Inspection, Monitoring and Evaluation

● "The Voluntary Organisation will co-operate with the Department's Inspection, Monitoring and Evaluation procedures."

It should be implicit in any contract that the local authority will expect to monitor the contracting organisation's performance and the contract should make explicit what is meant by this. Does the local authority intend to rely on the organisation's own evaluation processes or those which it undertakes in conjunction with a National Parent body? Does the local authority intend to carry out an evaluation according to a prescribed plan and if so, is this known to the voluntary organisation? It certainly should be. To what extent does the local authority intend to use consumer or user surveys as part of the process of monitoring and evaluation and if it does, who will organise this and pay for it and can it be shown to be effective and impartial?

How will it be determined that the quality and output of the voluntary organisation is adequate and how will any disputes or differences of judgement be determined?

What inspection arrangements are likely to be imposed or built into the monitoring and evaluation process? Will this be by the local authority or by a third party on behalf of the local authority? What are the expectations about access? If there are to be unannounced visits, is the voluntary organisation clear about the circumstances in which these may take place?

Food Safety Act

● "Voluntary organisations will ensure that any meals provided and any food preparation procedures are carried out in accordance with the requirement of the Food Safety Act and any regulations derived from it."

Recent regulation has imposed stringent legal requirements on organisations preparing and serving food. This is a responsibility which exists, irrespective of any contractual arrangements between a local authority and an organisation serving food, but the local authority may well wish to reinforce this legislation by making it a condition of the contract that the voluntary organisation complies. Clearly, any local authority that did not insist upon compliance in this respect would be in dereliction of its duty to its users.

Insurance

● "Voluntary organisations will at all times maintain, with a reputable insurance company, cover in an adequate sum to cover public liability, employers liability and fiduciary liability."

The importance of insurance cover can not be stressed too highly. It is an area where, in particular, smaller voluntary organisations are often deficient or sometimes there is merely a muddle in that it has not been determined whose responsibility it is to make sure that an insurance is taken out. Voluntary organisations also confuse their own responsibilities to take out insurance with that of the local authority's and assume that the local authority will take care of such matters.

The facts are that any organisation managing a service must be insured in its own right. Some insurance responsibilities are legally enforceable, for example, employers liability. It is therefore quite likely that a local authority will wish to spell out this responsibility in a contract and point the voluntary organisations attention to the need for public liability insurance which means that persons' interest is protected. Voluntary organisations would also be wise to take out fiduciary liability cover since unfortunately it is not unknown for members of staff of voluntary organisations as in the public service and in the world of commerce, to prove dishonest.

Annual Reports

● "The voluntary organisation will submit its annual report and audited accounts to the Council."

This, in a sense, reminds organisations that they should produce an annual report and that they should have their accounts audited and that it is reasonable for both to be sent to a major funder. An annual report is in any event an opportunity for a voluntary organisation to publicise what it is contributing and the discipline of producing such a report can of itself be a useful reflective exercise. Accounts auditing does not mean necessarily engaging in expensive accounting practices although if an organisation has a substantial turnover and particularly if it is a limited company, then it will need to engage a proper accountant. For smaller organisations, all that is necessary is that their records and accounts are verified by a competent person in good standing.

Access to Records

● "Voluntary organisations will allow inspection of its financial records and minute books by Council officers if requested with reasonable notice."

Some local authorities will insist on a clause of this nature. They will want their own access to an organisations financial records in order that, if necessary, they can carry out their own audit to ensure that affairs are being well managed. Some voluntary organisations may be resistant to giving this power and the sustainable argument would be that if the local authority has sufficient opportunity for ensuring that the service itself is being delivered as specified, there is no reason for the local authority to look specifically at its records or its minute books which may well contain confidential information.

Failure to Provide the Service

● "Voluntary organisations will notify the Council if for any reason it is unable to provide the service specified."

Any local authority will want to know if there is to be a break in the service. The question is, what are they likely to do about it? In a substantial contract with a well endowed voluntary organisation, for example a Housing Association, then the contract might in fact provide that it is the voluntary organisation's responsibility to make alternative arrangements to provide a service if it is having difficulties in providing the service itself. Such arrangements would be made at the voluntary organisation's own expense.

This is however precisely the sort of difficulty which is likely to inhibit smaller, less well funded and capitalised organisations to fear entering into a contractual obligation at all. For these organisations the local authority should be realistic and the arrangement should be that if there are difficulties in sustaining the service which cannot be resolved by discussion and support from the local authority, then the payments to be made should be renegotiated. An effective and sympathetic way of capturing this would be in a clause which would say something like the following:

> "Voluntary organisations will notify the Council if for any reason they are unable to provide the service as specified and will return such part of any unspent monies as the council may determine having regard to the voluntary organisations continuing commitments during a period of reduced service provision or their winding up costs in the event of the agreement needing to be terminated".

Nominated Officer

● "Voluntary organisations will co-operate and liaise with any specific officer of the Council that shall be appointed for this purpose."

We have spoken elsewhere of the importance of effective links being maintained between the contracting organisation and the local authority commissioning the contract. This may be considered to be so self-evident and important, that it does not need to be specifically written into an agreement.

The advantages of writing it into an agreement however is that the purpose is clearly recorded. It therefore supports the linkage and can in fact be used by the voluntary organisation as a claim against the local authority to provide for that liaison in those cases where perhaps other pressures are in danger of reducing it.

Equal Opportunities

- "Voluntary organisations will be required to operate an equal opportunities policy and practices affecting recruitment and the delivery of its services to the satisfaction of the Council."

The voluntary movement is usually strong on the need for equal opportunities in policy and in practice but there is every reason to spell this out within the context of a contract because, as with so many other elements which we are addressing requiring action by the voluntary organisation contracting, they do imply costs. It is more costly for an organisation to operate an equal opportunities policy than for it not to do so. At the simplest level, it can mean additional costs of advertising vacancies to ensure that they are read by members of the ethnic minority communities. At the more substantial level, it may mean considerable adaptation to buildings in order to make them accessible to people with disabilities. In so far as these factors are recorded in a contract, it therefore seems reasonable to expect the local authority to take these into account in its financial package.

Vehicle Safety

- "The voluntary organisation will ensure that any vehicles used to convey passengers satisfy legal safety standards."

It is again imperative that local authorities secure the safety of the users of services which they are paying for and sometimes the need for economies in the voluntary sector can mean that an attempt is made to cut costs on transport. Vehicles may not be well maintained and offers of help from volunteers with totally unsuitable cars may be accepted where it would be better to decline politely. Spelling these requirements out in a contract therefore can not only be a continuing reminder to voluntary organisations of their responsibilities and of the local authority's expectations but can be a mechanism used by the voluntary organisation itself to control the behaviour of its more reckless employees or volunteers.

Record Keeping

● "Voluntary organisations shall keep minutes of meetings and records of work undertaken including details of referrals, grounds for refusal, waiting lists etc. to indicate the nature and quality of work carried out."

As part of the monitoring of the agreement, a local authority will need information about the use which is being made of a service and it may want to indicate to the voluntary organisation the nature of the statistical information which should be collected. It is similarly important that details of referrals which can not be met should be recorded in order to add to the pool of information about unmet need. Voluntary organisations will no doubt wish to contribute to developing information about needs existing in the community which are not being met but sometimes they need reminding that this has to be collected and maintained as hard data rather than an impressionistic evidence.

Working with Children

● "Voluntary organisation will provide the Council with the names and personal details of staff and volunteers who it intends employing to work with children."

This will be for the purpose of checking with the Police the existence of any criminal convictions, the details of which will be given to the voluntary organisation. The voluntary organisation should notify the Council of its subsequent decision in relation to the employment of the person concerned. It is imperative that local authorities safeguard the interests of young people who may be receiving a service from a voluntary organisation on the Council's behalf. While, when people are being considered for employment, checking criminal convictions is not sufficient guarantee that they are not a potential danger, it must be an essential first step in a chain of investigations. The Police now make facilities available to local authorities for checking on whether individuals have convictions but often these facilities are not directly available to voluntary organisations themselves. It is an essential area therefore for co-operation.

Complaints Procedures

● "Voluntary organisation will maintain a procedure for receiving and investigating complaints."

Local authorities can all be expected to have their own complaints procedures and indeed Social Services departments have a statutory duty to have such processes.

This is all part of the move to develop services which are responsive to consumer and user needs and it seems equally relevant that the opportunity to complain should be available to people whose services are provided through a voluntary organisation. Some voluntary organisations may take the view that because they are community based and community led, they do not have the need for formal systems. This is not a sustainable argument. It is difficult enough for people to develop the courage to express negative feelings about a service which they are receiving without the processes for doing so being blurred. It is therefore a perfectly reasonable expectation of a local authority from a voluntary organisation providing contracted services to it that the voluntary organisation should have a clear well publicised system for dealing with complaints. Indeed it should be part of the local authority's monitoring and review systems to look at to what extent they have been used and what the response of the voluntary organisation was to complaints made. Complaints procedures do not have to be constructed in an entirely negative fashion of course; they can be incorporated with processes which encourage users and consumers to make comments on the service which they have received, both positive and of a complaining nature.

Personnel Policies

● "Voluntary organisation will provide details of its policies for recruiting, training, supporting and disciplining staff."

The quality and effectiveness of a voluntary organisations services will largely depend upon the quality and effectiveness of the staff it employs, whether they be paid or voluntary.

How a voluntary organisation deals with these issues is therefore of crucial importance to a local authority. Some authorities will therefore indicate in their contracts that the organisation has an ongoing responsibility to keep the local authority informed of any changes to its procedures. It should be mentioned however that local authorities may have only limited power to prescribe how a voluntary organisation treat their staff, since the 1988 Local Government Act appears to give a contracting organisation discretion over how many staff it uses to carry out particular parts of a specification and to have sole discretion over the conditions of service upon which it engages them.

Charging Policies

● "Voluntary organisation will indicate its charging policies to the Council."

In a mixed economy of care, it is important that what users who rely on state support pay for their services are broadly equitable. These issues are complicated and may well be dealt with most effectively within the framework of a local authority's care management system. Here a users ability to contribute towards a package of care is likely to be assessed on a once and for all basis and any contributions made by the user would be made direct to the local authority. The local authority would then meet any daily charges which were levied by a voluntary organisation. Clearly, if a voluntary organisation is being supported by a local authority through a block contract, issues about any residual daily or incremental charging should be worked out in advance since it is otherwise likely to become a source of contention.

User Involvement

● "Voluntary organisation will take into account the views of users in the development of its services."

Again, local authorities have a duty to ensure that the services which they pay for are user responsive. They should do this by ensuring that before they agree to pay for a service at all, it is a service which is acceptable to those who will rely upon it. But local authorities should also make clear that they have an ongoing expectation of a voluntary organisation that the service will constantly be adapted and fine tuned in line with the needs and wishes of those for whom it is for. Voluntary organisations are usually quite good at this but there is no harm in spelling it out clearly.

Carer Involvement

● "Voluntary organisation will take into account the views of carers in the development of its services."

Similar arguments apply on behalf of carers although this is a little bit more tricky since it is possible that the views and needs of carers could be in conflict with the needs and views of users. Nevertheless, local authorities through the Community Care Legislation have a duty to take into account the needs of carers and many may wish to emphasise this in the context of their contracts with voluntary organisations.

Quality Assurance

● "Voluntary organisation should implement a Quality Assurance Scheme."

Some local authorities are asking voluntary organisations to introduce formal schemes for quality assurance. One gets the impression that this might be a generalised statement of good intent without either the voluntary organisation or the local authority necessarily knowing precisely what is meant. Quality Assurance originally developed in highly technical industries where it was important that processes were carried out to very tight specifications in order to ensure that the desired outcome was "the same every time". It is important to understand that the desired outcome was capable of very tight definition. Applying these concepts in the service and welfare industries has proved quite difficult.

If local authorities require quality assurance therefore, it is important that they spell out what this means. If, for an extreme example, it intends that the voluntary organisation should be registered to British Standard 5750, then it must take into account that pursuing such a registration will impose considerable costs on the voluntary organisation and that few, if any, have already achieved this. If its expectations do not extend that far, then it needs to say how far they do extend. Similarly, there is sometimes a difficulty in definition. A quality assurance scheme is about producing a defined product consistently. It can sometimes be confused with determining what the product should look like. The distinction between requiring a quality assurance scheme and the determining of the product or standards, must therefore be separated.

Acknowledging the Council's Financial Contribution

● "Voluntary organisation will publicise the Council's financial support on its literature and in its accounts."

If local authorities do move wholesale into being enablers rather than direct providers of services, then it is to be expected that they will need to seek different mechanisms for ensuring that the public are aware of which services they have been responsible for. It is not uncommon therefore that voluntary organisations should be asked to acknowledge any financial contribution from a Council where the service being provided by the voluntary organisation is funded by the Council.

Representation on Management Committees

● "Voluntary organisation will ensure that the Council is invited to nominate a member to serve on its Management Committee."

This is a common condition which local authorities impose upon voluntary organisations but it is one which is subject to debate. On the one hand, it is clearly important, as we have already discussed, for there to be consistent liaison between a Council and its voluntary sector contractors. However some authorities are now having reservations about the efficacy and indeed propriety of insisting that their staff should serve on Management Committees. If someone sits on the Management Committee of a voluntary organisation their first loyalty in law is to the voluntary organisation itself. This can create a conflict of loyalty for a representative from a local authority who has what the Council may see as a prior responsibility to the Council itself. Such representation also compromises the voluntary organisation who may on occasions wish to discuss in confidence its relationship with the local authority. This could arise in the context of developing a negotiating position in which case it is quite inappropriate for the local authority to be party to the discussions. Therefore it is not recommended that local authorities should seek representation on the Committees of organisations who act as their contractors.

Chapter 7

The Local Authority's Commitment to its Voluntary Sector Contractors

We have looked in some detail at the expectations which a local authority may have of its voluntary sector contractors. We should now consider the commitments and obligations which the local authority has towards those contractors. Clearly, the largest contribution which the local authority will make will be the funding which it agrees to make available to enable the voluntary organisation to carry out the terms of the agreement. What attitude should a local authority take towards this sum?

The Price to be Paid

Voluntary organisations will seldom be in a position to call upon substantial reserves, particularly if they are local or small. It is important therefore that the local authority does not seek to screw voluntary organisations to the wall when it is negotiating the financial package. The financial assessment of a potential contractor will always form part of the pre-assessment process which a local authority will carry out and it should seek at this stage to ascertain that the voluntary organisation is able to deliver the service specified for the payment to be agreed. The discussion about this payment should be honest and open; there is no point in a local authority seeking to sneak a financial advantage if the voluntary organisation concerned appears to be weak on negotiating skills or naive about the financial consequences of its commitment. If the voluntary organisation is naive to the point of managerial incompetence, then it may be preferable for the local authority not to deal with it. But if, as is more likely to be the case, it has simply not considered all the factors which bear on its future costings, then it is much better that the local authority calls attention to this.

This could be complicated of course if the negotiation of the specific contract is taking place following a process of competitive tendering where the scope for post tender negotiation is more limited. The objective must however always be to ensure that there is a realistic probability that the organisation will be able to carry out the service contracted for the money to be transferred. If there is any doubt about this it should be clear what the mechanism for dealing with any problems will be.

Joint or Partial Funding

One area of uncertainty which may arise is where a voluntary organisation is seeking joint funding for an activity which is indivisible. A day centre for elderly mentally infirm people may be an activity towards which both Health and Social Services accept a responsibility for contributing, but which neither are prepared to pay for outright. A simple solution is for the voluntary organisation to have a joint contract with both authorities but if the Health Authority were not prepared to enter into such an obligation, then there may need to be provision in the contract with the local authority for either side to withdraw from the arrangement if the Health Authority's funding fails. Another example could be where a service is heavily dependent upon good will over the use of the building or the involvement of voluntary workers. Clearly, if a building was no longer available or if the voluntary workers withdrew their services, then the voluntary organisations ability to deliver would be jeopardised.

In Oxfordshire, this difficulty has been circumvented in such circumstances by a clause which states:

"The Local Authority recognises that the voluntary organisation's ability to sustain the service as specified depends upon it continuing to attract the facilities and support of other organisations and volunteers and that if these are withdrawn, its ability to provide the service will be jeopardised which shall entitle either the voluntary organisation or the local authority to terminate this agreement".

Clauses such as this may in one sense be seen as weakening the effectiveness of the contract for securing a service at a fixed cost on a long term basis but in my view this is more than offset by the trust and good will which can be developed as a result of taking a more realistic approach. It is basically the difference between an approach which draws on the ethos, skills and expertise of community development rather than a more legalistic duties based approach taken from commercial contracting.

Contract Monitoring

The ethos which a local authority adopts for its voluntary sector contracting will nowhere be more apparent than in the attitude it takes towards monitoring its contracts with voluntary organisations. Early experiences appear to indicate that those local authorities that draw their expertise for contracting with the voluntary sector from their experiences of dealing with compulsory competitive tendering are much more difficult for the voluntary sector to relate to.

These departments tend to produce their specifications without too much consultation, seek tenders and offer contracts to those who appear to be most cost effective. The contracts are then monitored through professional contract managing departments in a way which seeks to ensure compliance at all times with the letter of the contract with quick moves towards seeking redress if things go amiss. This sort of approach may be useful for monitoring a contract with a commercial organisation providing refuse services but it is unlikely to get the best out of the voluntary sector.

Most voluntary organisations are simply not equipped either financially or in terms of expertise and personnel to deal with a local authority which adopts such a hard nosed approach. It is likely therefore that the only voluntary organisations that would be able to relate to the process would be those large national organisations that do have considerable resources and which to all intents and purposes must be seen as the non-profit making equivalent of commercial companies. They are unlikely to be locally based organisations and their sole presence in "the market" will amplify the suspicions and worries in the voluntary sector that contracting will lead to the demise of the smaller local organisations with its heavy commitment to user involvement and the provision of a service which is tailor-made to the needs of particular localities.

Partnerships

My own preference therefore is that local authorities should develop a softer partnership approach in contracting with voluntary organisations.

This in turn means that legal departments, whilst having an essential advisory role to play, should be put somewhat in a supportive rather than a leading role. In a number of authorities, individual agreements with voluntary organisations are drawn up with officers without reference to the legal department apart from an initial involvement in advising on the kind of agreement to be used. This is more cost effective for the local authorities concerned and least threatening to the voluntary sector who in turn may find it difficult to afford legal advice at all.

Needless to say, in complex contracts for large sums of money and particularly for the provision of residential services, sufficient care must be taken by both voluntary and statutory body to ensure that they have an agreement which can stand the test of time and changes in personnel. Today's trusting partners may not be around tomorrow. If however the local authority is clear that its objective is essentially to bring clarity into the relationship. If it is clear about how much money it can afford to spend, and this means avoiding giving false hopes about how much money might be available next year; if it is clear about the circumstances in which an agreement should be terminated and the mechanisms for doing so, then contracting does not have to be difficult for either party. If furthermore, the local authority's attitude towards its contractors is that it is seeking to build lasting long term partnerships to provide quality care cost effectively, then it seems to me that it can build a relationship with the voluntary organisations it does business with which allows it to support them in carrying out their own obligations.

Working at Both Ends of the Contract

The approach I am advocating can be described as working at both ends of the contract. At the local authority end, contract management and monitoring processes, as we shall discuss later, are firm and explicit. They indicate a determination to see the service delivered as specified and to the quality standards agreed. At the voluntary organisations end however, there is a recognition by the local authority that the contractor, particularly if it is a smallish voluntary organisation, does not have access to the wide range of support mechanisms and systems which are available to local authority providers.

Similarly, this approach recognises that during the grants

culture, local authorities did significantly more for their voluntary organisations than give grant aid. They often provided buildings, help with transport, participation in training events, as well as providing management advice when asked to do so. Such support is even more necessary to a voluntary organisation as a contractor. As a result of the very contract, expectations on them will run higher and their management task and responsibilities will be clearer.

Support for Local Development Agencies

In local authorities which are trying to develop best practice efforts are being made to reinforce the management of voluntary organisations. In Oxfordshire, as an example, this is happening directly and indirectly.

Indirectly the County Council is seeking to reinforce the voluntary sector by having long term agreements with Councils for Voluntary Action, Volunteer Bureaus and other organisations fulfilling local development agency functions such as the County Branch of Age Concern with the expectation that these organisations will support other voluntary organisations through the contracting process. This therefore is about supporting and reinforcing the voluntary sector infrastructure and it is extremely important that this should happen in order that voluntary organisations should have access to independent support systems. Unfortunately, in some parts of the country, this is an activity which the move to contracting has diminished. In my view it arises out of a too narrow interpretation of what the contract culture is about.

Local authorities which focus only on those organisations which are capable of providing an explicit service to clients are likely to find that their local voluntary sector infrastructure is weakened and in future they will have to deal either with national voluntary organisations, whose presence can sometimes be deeply resented by local voluntary groups who can not themselves obtain financial support, or by the commercial sector. It is a danger which local authorities are strongly urged to guard against. The Community Care Act calls attention to the need for local authorities to develop a market in community care where one is not otherwise available and one way of seeking to achieve this is by reinforcing the voluntary sector in the way described.

Direct Support with Training, Advice and Consultancy

At a second level however, local authorities can give direct support to their service contractors.

For example, many contracts may require voluntary organisations to have adequate insurance policies, quality assurance schemes, equal opportunities policies, pay attention to new legal requirements, for example the Food Safety Act, and yet the organisations themselves may only have a very rudimentary idea of what all this entails. We all know that attending national training courses on these issues is a very expensive business and may be beyond the financial abilities of the average voluntary organisation with a £50,000-£100,000 turnover. Local authorities need to provide this training in-house for their own staff all the time and it seems reasonable that they should include provision for their voluntary sector partners. Not only does this mean that training can be provided more cost effectively but it also means that there are opportunities created for providers in the voluntary sector to rub shoulders with those who still remain in the public sector. Both can learn from the experiences, difficulties and values of the other.

Furthermore, voluntary organisations will often need management advice and access to professional expertise. Again, consultancy is extremely expensive and unless the local authority's contract has provided an income to the voluntary organisation to buy this in, it again seems reasonable that the local authority should open up its own systems to the voluntary sector.

The provision of direct resources is perhaps a little more tricky but it would be a foolish contract which did not provide for the independent provider to approach its local authority purchaser if it was running into real difficulties over questions of accommodation or transport for example.

Some agreements provide for voluntary organisations to buy back into the local authority's transport arrangements and many rent buildings from local authorities.

Dangers to Avoid

It is not that one is trying to be too prescriptive in this area but simply to convey a style of dealing with voluntary sector providers which recognises their value systems and financial realities and seeks to develop a partnership and trust within a context of determination to seek good quality services. In my view, the consequences of not going down this route may be serious It could mean that arbitrary distinctions could be built into the purchaser/contractor relationship leading to expertise and experience not being readily transferred from one side of the equation to the other. It could lead to a reluctance by the voluntary sector to feel that they have a part to play in contracting with the local authorities and in particular, it could lead to shutting out the more informally organised local organisations with a commensurate loss of the rich expertise and added value which they contribute to community life. It could herald a failure of local authorities to be seen pursuing their responsibilities for developing an alternative range of independent provision and it could ultimately lead to the concentration of services in the hands of a small group of commercial bureaucracies which would have no more to commend them than the local authority monopolies which according to Government have been found wanting.

Chapter 8
Monitoring Contracts

It will be clear by now that I favour contracts which are clear on specification, strong on spelling out the local authority's management expectations of an organisation with a contract, and user friendly. They should also spell out the local authority's determination to enable the voluntary organisation to deliver the service required. The monitoring process will however be thorough and the local authority will appoint a Contract Manager for each contract with the voluntary sector. This person will hopefully have both a good understanding of the service which the voluntary organisation is trying to deliver and also an empathy towards voluntary organisations as providers. He or she will however be equally clear of their responsibilities to the local authority and to the users of the service for ensuring that they do get the service which is being paid for. The Contract Manager should be well known to the voluntary organisation and should maintain frequent contact. This contact should not be intrusive but neither should it be spurious. The Contract Manager has a job to do and this is to ensure that any problems are quickly made visible and dealt with.

The monitoring process can be broken down into a number of components which we may look at in turn.

Compliance Monitoring

Let us assume that we have our agreement/contract. It contains a specification which is sufficiently detailed to describe the service which is being provided by the voluntary organisation and contains details of the requirements which the local authority is making of the organisation in terms of its management.

Compliance Monitoring then sets about investigating whether everything is being done as agreed. The appointed officer will want to check that the conservation group with a contract to keep a recreation ground tidy has in fact kept the grass cut below the specified 4 inches, that the trees have been pruned and the newly planted shrubs were watered. He/she will check that the volunteers who carried out the work of clearing the pond were provided with suitable waterproof clothing and that they were given training in the use of chainsaws and eye protection and ear muffs when they lobbed the willows at the edge.

Compliance Monitoring will check that the day centre was open on the days when the contract said it would be open and that there were sufficient staff there to cope with the numbers of people who were expected. That a nourishing meal was provided at midday and that the transport arrived on time to take the elderly people home. Compliance Monitoring is simply looking at what is objective, what is agreed and enquiring whether it has been done. It is an ongoing process and should entail regular contacts between the officer responsible for the links with the voluntary organisation and the responsible persons in the voluntary organisation. The Contract Manager should develop a systematic process for liaising with the project and for getting feed back from appropriate sources. These sources will include the users themselves and representatives of the users as well as from any professional workers who are responsible for referring potential users to the project or who build the use of a particular facility into a care plan.

The Contract Manager should feel no sense of unease at asking to see records and to receive details of unmet needs or waiting lists. This should nevertheless be a dynamic process, the Contract Manager should seek to ensure that problems encountered are resolved speedily. There is no point in storing problems up for the annual review if dissatisfaction is expressed that perhaps a facility does not open as regularly as it should or it does not provide the range of services which the users or their carers have come to expect. The reasons for this must be promptly investigated and the voluntary organisation given an opportunity to put things right.

Standards/Quality

It may not always be possible or practicable to deal with all issues concerning standards or quality in a specification. The issues may be too complex or too indeterminate. If there is considerable trust between the parties, it may not even have been considered necessary to spell these issues out in any great detail.

The monitoring process should however try to determine what standards or quality has been achieved. If an organisation has a formal quality assurance scheme, is this working? Who has checked? Has the organisation checked itself or has it been audited by some third party? Does the voluntary organisation follow agreed codes of practice perhaps because it is part of a wider network or has some parent organisation? If so, are the codes of practice being clearly adhered to?

There may be issues about new standards being set by government regulatory bodies, by advisory bodies within quangos, the voluntary sector itself or by local authorities? How do these standards relate to the reality of the service which is being provided in this situation? If the standards are not being attained, is this because they are unrealistic or because of constraints to do with training, physical environment or financial resources? If so, how will these issues be dealt with? There can be issues to do with quality which may be quite subjective. A service contract for example may indicate that the voluntary organisation should provide a nourishing meal but there is a certain subjective element in determining what a nourishing meal might be. Issues such as this need to be addressed and reconciled.

Customer Surveys

One fairly objective mechanism for monitoring a service is to ask the users standard questions about it. The users of an organisation providing community meals for example might be asked whether the choice offered is to their liking. Whether it arrives at a good temperature. Whether the time it is delivered is suitable to them or not. They might be asked if they can afford to pay what they are charged without hardship or similarly whether they would be willing to pay more for a better quality meal.

Customer surveys can be a very useful mechanism for determining what customers think of a particular service and also for making comparisons between services provided by different organisations whether in the voluntary, private or public sector.

Inspection

Inspection should be seen as a specific process which has its own distinctive part to play in any monitoring arrangements. Monitoring is not only about inspection, and inspection is only a part of monitoring. Inspections are about looking at a particular aspect of a service in some detail to see whether it is working on a particular day. Inspections therefore are often unannounced, in other words those to be inspected are not aware of when the inspection will take place, though not all inspections need to be like that.

In the new Community Care Legislation the place of inspection is given particular prominence and local authorities are instructed to establish inspection units which are at arms length from the local authority. These units will have responsibility for inspecting the quality of care provided not only in establishments in the private and voluntary sector but also those provided directly by the local authority.

It is quite likely that these arms length inspection units will have their functions extended over time until they cover all aspects of the work of local authority Social Services departments.

One of the aims of inspection is to ascertain the effectiveness of other monitoring functions, for example the way the monitoring officer carries out his/her role, and also to compare the quality of care being provided over a range of different facilities. It seems important that standards operating within a local authority area should be consistently applied across all of the local authorities contractors.

Performance Indicators

Monitoring should look at outcomes as well as inputs and outputs. Performance Indicators are one way of measuring this. We all use performance indicators in our daily routines; if we buy a new car we will enquire how fast it can move from 0 – 60 mph and how many miles to a gallon of fuel it can achieve. If we buy a light bulb, we will want to know how long it is likely to last. These are performance indicators and although we may not be used to applying them to the work of voluntary organisations, they are very much with us.

Part of the monitoring process therefore should be to establish performance indicators which can form fair and objective criteria for judging how well an organisation has performed. If the objectives of a day centre are to prevent elderly people needing to be received into residential care, then the organisation and the local authority may wish to measure how many of the users actually end up in residential care. If the objective of the day centre is to maintain 90% capacity, then again those monitoring would need to know whether it achieved that target or whether it did better or worse. It is important when setting performance indicators not to overwhelm a voluntary organisation with too many; better to take half a dozen and stick to them rather than taking two dozen and then fail to measure whether they have been achieved or not because of the burden of collecting all the relevant statistics.

Self Evaluation

It is often said that the aim of all evaluation processes is to turn them into self evaluation. We have already mentioned quality assurance systems and the need where they are in operation for the organisation using them to check how effectively they are working; that is a form of self evaluation. But organisations need constantly to be looking at their objectives and whether they are still valid. They need to examine the activities which they organise in furtherance of their objectives and the effectiveness of those activities both in terms of cost and appropriateness to meet the objectives stated. This involves looking at the role of management committees, paid and volunteer staff, how they interrelate and how well the organisation manages itself to ensure that all parts are pulling in the same direction.

Some organisations are quite fastidious about carrying out self evaluation. It is not cheap since it absorbs resources but neither is it expensive when placed against the organisational costs of not doing it. Where voluntary organisations are seen to have effective systems for self monitoring, then the local authority Contract Manager will bolt onto them and his/her own activities can become more of the order of verifying the effectiveness of the self evaluation process.

Review/Audit

The monitoring process is ongoing but it is going to be important in the lifetime of any contract to take stock. To carry out an audit of what has been happening.

This will be necessary, not only for the purpose of comparing understandings of how well the organisation is doing as a contractor but also to prepare the ground for decisions about the future of the contract. The Contract Manager must clearly be involved in this process on behalf of the local authority but it can be useful to involve a third party, either a colleague from another part of the organisation or even an independent consultant. The role of this third party may be to act as a facilitator to the process to ensure that the right questions are asked. In authorities where there is a willingness to roll contracts on, then it is appropriate to carry out a review\audit on an annual basis in order that the decision can be made about whether the contract is in fact to be rolled on. There may be two constraints on a contract being rolled on. The first to do with the local authority's perceptions about how far and how competently the voluntary sector contractor has carried out the service in accordance with the specification and management requirements. Then secondly, a separate judgement has to be made about whether the service is still the most appropriate way of meeting need. We are all familiar with the syndrome of services being provided year on year without much regard to changing circumstances and without perhaps enquiring too assiduously whether there are better ways of meeting the needs of the people targeted. The future is likely to be more dynamic and changing than the past and local authorities will wish to modify the services which they offer in line with changing views and perceptions by users of their own needs.

The rolling contract can provide a mechanism for addressing these needs since at the point where a decision has to be made about whether the contract should be rolled on, the local authority must discuss honestly with the voluntary organisation, if they feel that the service being offered is becoming a lower priority. The voluntary organisation then has three choices. It can use the time remaining to wind down its activities. It can discuss with the local authority and the service users how it may play a part in offering a different kind of service which matches the new requirements expressed. Or, it can decide to seek alternative funding to carry on providing a service which it believes is important even if the local authority does not.

On the other hand, the review\audit does offer the opportunity to make other kinds of decisions too. The review may be the appropriate moment to identify that the service being provided does in fact need to expand or that the payment being offered by the local authority is not sufficient in changing circumstances to maintain the existing service at an appropriate level. The reviewing officer should then indicate to the voluntary organisation what steps will be taken to seek additional funding or if this is not feasible, consider how the service must be reshaped to match the resources which are available.

It can be seen that the monitoring process is an absolutely vital part of the contracting process. If it is carried out thoroughly and seen as an ongoing commitment by both sides, then it provides a mechanism for dealing promptly with problems and difficulties as they arise in order that surprises may be avoided. There should not be too many surprises at the review!

A consumer survey should not be too startling in its revelations about the users' perceptions of the service which they are receiving. An inspection whether announced or unannounced should not be too devastating. It has to be said of course that effective monitoring takes time, takes patience, it takes commitment, it takes skill and experience. It must however be acknowledged that experience can only be won through the passage of time and the place of patience is to allow this time to pass in order that maturity over monitoring can develop. What is imperative is that all aspects of what I have described as the monitoring process should be seen to play their part and that in particular, every attempt should be made to ensure that the monitoring process is not orientated and orchestrated on the basis of a need to find fault.

If the voluntary sector come to feel that the local authority's monitoring processes are about trying to catch them out, then they will be rightly distrustful of the process and of those involved in it. Their co-operation will be less than fulsome and they will develop techniques for disguising problems which need to be exposed and dealt with. There will of course be problems and some of them will be problems which may not be capable of resolution. If a voluntary organisation loses all of its volunteers or the commitment of its Management Committee; if the building it uses falls down and an alternative can not be found; if the cost of providing a particular service escalates beyond the control of the organisation and the capacity of the local authority to respond with new money then a service may have to be terminated.

Equally, if a voluntary organisation is not able to control its operations, if it appoints poor quality staff and fails to train and support them, if it is unable to develop good team working or deal with conflicts and personality clashes, then the local authority may decide that the service is just not good enough.

Even so, it is important that the arrangements for termination should be fair and not punishment orientated and that they should allow for the business to be wound up with as little loss of face and acrimony as is possible. In their dealings with voluntary organisations, local authorities should recognise that it will seldom be expedient or sensible to resort to court action and that it will usually be preferable to seek to cut any loses and leave a door open for re-building bridges in the future.

Chapter 9
Review and Conclusions

Since the Contract Culture is a fact, it seems sensible to make it work to the benefit of the parties concerned. There are advantages to contracting if the approach includes a genuine desire to bring clarity into a relationship with a voluntary organisation and to develop that relationship as an honest and effective partnership with the hope that it will be long lasting. Whilst concerns that the service should be economical *vis-à-vis* alternatives will clearly be a factor in striking an ultimate bargain, it should be recognised by local authorities that contracting is not necessarily of itself, a route to cheapness.

It has been pointed out however, that the voluntary sector has many reservations about engaging in contracting with local authorities and that these reservations and concerns have to be honestly addressed from the word go. They are more capable of being resolved if the local authority is clear about its own objectives and is willing to discuss the voluntary sectors concerns both in general terms in relation to specific contracts. We have also seen that the introduction of contracting is likely to be quite dramatic for the average local authority. It will necessitate them rethinking how they use their staff, who are the purchasers and who are the providers. Local authorities will need to consider the place of their legal departments and their accountants and they will need to determine who can negotiate and who can make decisions. The ultimate decision of course is the decision about who has the authority to sign the contract. We have said that it is useful to share with voluntary organisations these dilemmas within the local authority in order that the voluntary sector can see that the issues about contracting are just as complex for local authorities as they are for voluntary organisations.

We have, nevertheless, taken the stand that there is no alternative but to face and reconcile the difficulties about contracting if there is to be much of a future in the relationship between voluntary organisations and local authorities. New legislation and financial constraints on local authorities make it inevitable that in future they will have to keep tighter count of any monies which they use and this means not only being fairly specific about how it is to be used but also quite diligent in seeing that it is used wisely.

We have therefore concluded that it is imperative that voluntary organisations and local authorities work together on developing mechanisms which can ensure that the contracting process is in the best interests of the users of services. We can summarise these processes as follows and refer to the types of tools which may be developed for facilitating it.

Assessing Potential Contractors

Once a local authority has decided its priorities for service deliver, it will be in a position to decide how the service should be commissioned. It basically has two options.

1. To provide directly.

2. To contract the service out.

If it chooses the latter course, then it has to identify a supplier. It may do this via a tendering process or by direct negotiation but at some point it must audit any organisation likely to be chosen to ascertain its competence and stability. Local authorities therefore need to develop a process for this involving relevant professional and technical expertise.

Draft specification documents are useful tools to assist in this process and have been developed in a number of authorities. Questionnaires can also be produced to ascertain an organisation's attitudes to, for example, recruitment and employment, equal opportunities, training, or to discover what experiences it has of service delivery. The work of drafting such questionnaires, in fact, offers opportunities for colleagues in health and social services to work in collaboration with the voluntary sector and users and carers. There must also be opportunities for teams auditing the suitability of potential providers to be multi-disciplinary.

Drawing up the Contract

We have suggested that the technical job of producing the contract should be made as simple as practicable. We have considered in detail what it might contain and said that for all but the most complex contracts which will need a solicitor, it is likely that pro formas can be used and we have suggested that these should be produced as tools in conjunction with the voluntary sector itself. Appendix 1. is an example of such a tool or checklist. It is used in Oxfordshire and was designed in conjunction with voluntary organisations. It provides both the potential contractor and the negotiators from the department with guidance as to the eventual content of the contract and details those requirements which are essential.

Responses to the questions prompted by the checklist can be converted into statements which appear as clauses in the agreement and which are chosen from a pro forma. This is made available on disc to Officers throughout the Department who may only occasionally be producing contracts. It helps them to produce documents for signature which are accurate and framed in accordance with the department's expectations and with the requirements of its legal advisors.

The Monitoring Stage

We have suggested that this should be a tough but fair process enabling rather than punishing. It should be based on the written agreement. If the agreement does not specify some aspects of service which the monitoring officer would like to see provided, it is too bad unless the voluntary organisation is ready to renegotiate the agreement. Contracts have to be used in this way if they are to do the job of bringing clarity rather than confusion into a relationship. Since it is quite possible that monitoring contracts will be a small part of the responsibilities of a wide number of officers in a local authority which does not have separate contracting sections, the disadvantages of which we have already discussed, tools will again be useful. A form, used for the annual review of a contract produced from the checklist illustrated at Appendix 1, asks such questions as:

Has the organisation delivered the service it agreed to deliver?

Has it managed itself in accordance with the local authority's requirements?

Has the local authority sent its cheques out on time and given any other support agreed?

If the answer to any of these questions is no, what remedial action has been taken or is proposed?

It then directs attention to the future and asks:

Should everything continue as it is?

Is any variation needed?

Should any further developments take place?

How is the funding for these to be secured?

It finally invites the voluntary organisation to make independent comments about the process of monitoring as they have experienced it.

It should be repeated that vital though the annual review is, it should produce no real surprises if the ongoing work of contract management has been effective. It is essential that regular contact is maintained between the local authority's appointed officer and the voluntary organisations staff and that problems are attended to as they occur and not stored up. Similarly the work of providing training to enable voluntary sector providers to update their skills and performance should be built into the local authority's training plans.

Finally ...

This book will hopefully be of practical use to voluntary organisations and statutory bodies developing contractual relationships with each other. If it has satisfied its authors intentions, its particular contribution to the development of the Contract Culture will be to show that the new culture must embrace vital elements of the old, in particular, the public service ethic and local authorities community development and leadership roles. It does not need to be seen on its own however and for the serious student of contracting, a reading list at Appendix V provides further guidance and food for thought.

OXFORDSHIRE COUNTY COUNCIL
Social Services Department
Service Agreement
Checklist and Form of Agreement

In the light of many changes which are affecting the way Local Authorities operate, and in particular because of the need to be clear about how public money is to be used, most funding from the Social Services Committee to voluntary organisations will in future be regulated through a service agreement. The purpose of the agreement will be to specify what the voluntary organisation will provide and its organisational responsibilities in providing it and to indicate the County Council's commitments. For each service agreement, a Manager from the Social Services department will be appointed to take the lead in negotiating and then monitoring the agreement with the support of the Principal Officer, Community Services. The voluntary organisation will appoint their own negotiators.

The following checklist can be used to assist in drawing up the agreement, the clauses written in bold italics refer to essential elements for all service agreements.

Introduction

This should indicate who the agreement is between and when it will commence. It should then state;

Whereby in consideration of the sum specified in C.1. the (voluntary organisation) agree:

A Service Specification

1. This should make clear precisely what it is that the voluntary organisation is going to do
   a. What is to be provided – can this be stated in general terms, e.g. daycare or specific terms i.e daycare for elderly/mentally infirm people with incontinence problems.
   b. Can the ingredients for service be further stated, i.e the service will incorporate offer of facilities for hairdressing, chiropody, bathing, meals and games.

c. What statements need to be made about the standards of the service, i.e a nourishing meal or a meal of a certain calorific value with defined contents of fat, fibre, etc and with a choice for people with different dietary needs.

d. Who is eligible to receive the service, i.e anyone. Is it restricted to certain age groups or people from particular localities? Is it clear that there are no restrictions on grounds of race?

e. How often is the service to be provided – number of weeks, days, hours open.

f. How is access to be obtained/determined, i.e through Social Service referrals or at discretion of voluntary organisations.

g. How much of the service will be provided, i.e how many meals will be served? How many people can be accommodated?

B Service Requirements

This section is intended to clarify the responsibilities of the voluntary organisation in delivering the service and should address the following issues;

a. Should there be a statement that the Voluntary Organisation will provide a safe system of work for the people working at the project, both paid and volunteer staff and for those using its facilities and shall have regard to the needs of disabled people.

b. Should any performance targets be specified – even as a minimum, e.g "will act in accordance with its national bodies' code of practice".

c. The (Voluntary Organisation) will co-operate with the Council's Inspection, Monitoring and Evaluation procedures which shall include:
   i. Consumer surveys
   ii. Compliance Monitoring
   iii. Consideration of an organisations record on staff recruitment and retention, training and development, and equal opportunities
   iv. Evaluation of quality and output

d. The (Voluntary Organisation) will be required to conduct its affairs in a reputable manner and observe all legal requirements.

e. The (voluntary organisation) will at all times maintain with a reputable insurance company, insurance cover in an adequate sum to cover public liability and if necessary employers liability.

f. The (Voluntary Organisation) will be required to submit its annual report and audited accounts to the Director of Social Services.

g. The (Voluntary Organisation) will be required to allow inspection of its books by Council Officers, at any reasonable time, if requested with 14 days notice.

h. The (Voluntary Organisation) will be required to notify the Director of Social Services, if for any reason it is unable to sustain the service as specified and will return such part of any unspent grant as the Council's Director of Social Services may determine having regard to:

   i. The organisations continuing commitments during a period of reduced service provision, or

   ii. Their winding up costs in the event of termination of the agreement

i. The (Voluntary Organisation) will be required to avoid incurring financial or other obligations it does not have the ability to meet.

j. Should the Voluntary Organisation be required to co-operate and liaise with any specified Officers of the Social Services Department.

k. Do any statements need to be made about the (Voluntary Organisation) charging policies?

l. State that the (Voluntary Organisation) will be required to operate an equal opportunities policy affecting recruitment to the satisfaction of the County Council.

m. Should the (Voluntary Organisation) be required to ensure that any vehicles used to convey passengers satisfy safety standards and are suitable for the clients being conveyed in them and should be comprehensively insured with a reputable insurance company.

n. The (Voluntary Organisation) will be required to keep minutes of meetings and records of work undertaken, including waiting lists if necessary to indicate the volume and the nature of the work being carried out.

o. Should the (Voluntary Organisation) be required to provide adequate care and/or supervision for any users of the service.

p. Should the (Voluntary Organisation) be required to maintain a procedure for receiving and investigating complaints, and keeping details of complaints received and how they were dealt with.

q. Should the (Voluntary Organisation) be required to indicate its staff recruitment, training, development supervisory and disciplinary procedures.

r. Should there be any requirements for the Voluntary Organisation to involve users of its services or their representatives on any decision making forum.

s. Should the voluntary organisation be required to consult with carers in respect of the services to be provided.

t. The Organisation will operate any food preparation, service or retail process in accordance with the requirements of the Food Safety Act and any regulations derived from it.

C The Council's Contribution

1. This Section should indicate what the Council will do for the voluntary organisation.

   a. Indicate the County Councils financial contribution, and how it will be paid, whether it is index linked and how any inflation would be decided.

   b. List any other Social Services department support to be provided e.g Premises, Transport, Training, Advice. The Council and the (voluntary organisation) acknowledge and agree that:

D General Conditions

This section indicates how long the agreement will last, review and termination arrangements and any other matters considered important.

   a. Should there be a statement that both the Voluntary Organisation and the County Council respect and acknowledge each others values.

   b. This agreement will be subject to an annual review which

will cover all aspects of the operation of the agreement. Further reviews may be requested by either side at any time. In the final year of the operation of the agreement the annual review will take place sufficiently early in the year to enable both sides to give the other 3 months notice of whether the agreement is to be continued.

The terms of this agreement may be varied by mutual consent.

c. The agreement will last for X years and end on (date).

d. State that the County Council cannot undertake to increase its grant aid without prior agreement and that any service additions must be planned on this understanding by the Voluntary Organisation.

e. Nothing herein contained shall limit/(the voluntary organisation) or the Council from pursuing any other lawful activity which they are empowered to pursue provided that the grant paid by the Council hereunder shall not be used for purposes which constitute a breach by the Council of part II of the Local Government Act 1986 (see Annex).

f. Should there be a statement that the County Council recognises that the (Voluntary Organisation's) ability to continue to provide the service depends upon it continuing to enjoy the financial support and/or facilities of other organisations or volunteers.

Also that if these are withdrawn, the (Voluntary Organisation's) ability to continue to provide the service will be jeopardized which should entitle either the (Voluntary Organisation) or the Council to terminate the agreement.

g. State that this Agreement can be terminated by three months notice served on the Director of Social Services by the Voluntary Organisation if they hold the County Council to be in breach of the terms of this agreement. Does this also need to state that the Voluntary Organisation can terminate the agreement on grounds of factors arising out of clause D (g.) if included.

h. This Agreement can be terminated by three months notice served on the Voluntary Organisation by the Council's Director of Social Services, if the Council holds the

Voluntary Organisation to be in breach of the terms of this agreement, provided this notice is endorsed by the Social Services Committee. If the Social Services Committee are being asked to consider a recommendation to give such changed approval to endorsement, then the Voluntary Organisation will be given an opportunity to submit their views to the Social Services Committee before a decision is reached. On giving such notice to terminate, the Council shall not be obliged to make any further payments and the (Voluntary Organisation) will not expend any further monies of the unspent grant on hand without the express consent of the Council's Director of Social Services.

i. Should this agreement be terminated the (Voluntary Organisation) shall pay forthwith to theCouncil, either a sum equivalent to a pro rata refund of the unspent grant proportionate to the unexpired period for which the grant or the particular instalment thereon was paid or the actual unspent grant, whichever shall be the greater.

Signed by	....	Signed by	....
Name	....	Name	....
Position	....	Position	....
For and on behalf of The County Council		For and on behalf of The Voluntary Organisation	
Date	....	Date	....
Witnessed by	....	Witnessed by	....
Signature	....	Signature	....
Name	....	Name	....
Address	....	Address	....
Date	....	Date	....

Reading List

Bidding for Change? Voluntary Organisations and Competitive
Tendering for Local Authority Services
by Christian Kunz , Rowan Jones, Ken Spencer

Partners or Agents
by Richard Gutch, Christian Kunz, Ken Spencer

Caring for People – Community Care in the Next Decade and
Beyond   *by HMSO*

Purchase of Service – Practical Guidance Social Services
Departments and other Agencies
by DHSS Inspectorate

Contracts for Social Care
by Association of Metropolitan Authorities

Quality and Contracts in the Personal Social Services
by Association of Metropolitan Authorities

Twelve Charity Contracts
by Anne Davis, Ken Edwards

Contracts at the Crossroads – Guidance for Voluntary and
Statutory Agencies in Negotiating Contracts
by Rodney Hedley, Colin Rochester

Contracting Lessons from the United States
by Richard Gutch

Getting Reading for Contracts – A Guide for Voluntary
Organisations   *by Sandy Adirondack, Richard MacFarland*

Contracting In or Out – A Series of Publications
by NCVO

These can all be obtained from the Directory of Social Change